New Heinemann Maths

6

Textbook

Heinemann

Heinemann is an imprint of Pearson Education Limited,
a company incorporated in England and Wales, having
its registered office at Edinburgh Gate, Harlow, Essex,
CM20 2JE. Registered company number: 872828

Heinemann is a registered trademark of Pearson Education Limited

Writing team
John T Blair
Percy W Farren
Myra A Pearson
John W Thayers
David K Thomson

First Published 2002

15
20

ISBN 978 0 435178 74 1

Typeset by Mandy Emery.
Illustrated by David Till, David Kearney, Derek Brazell,
Diane Fawcett, Tony O'Donnell and Jon Mitchell, .
Cover Illustation by Mark Oliver.
Printed and bound in China (CTPS/20)

Contents

	TEXTBOOK	EXTENSION TEXTBOOK
Place value		
Numbers with up to 8 digits	1	
Comparing and ordering	2	
Adding/subtracting multiples of powers of ten	3	
Multiplying/dividing by 10, 100, 1000	4	
Using and applying, estimating	5	
Rounding	6	
		E1
Addition		
Of several two-digit numbers	7	
Of three-digit numbers, bridging a multiple of 10	8	
Of three-digit numbers, bridging a multiple of 100	9	
Of three-digit numbers, bridging 1000	10	
Of four-digit numbers, no bridging/bridging a multiple of 10	11	
Of four-/five-digit numbers, standard written method	12	
Of numbers with up to five digits, standard written method	13	
Using and applying, calculator	14	
Subtraction		
Of three-digit multiples of 10	15	
Of a three-digit number from a three-digit multiple of 10	16	
Of three-digit numbers, bridging a multiple of 10	17	
Of three-/four-digit numbers, no bridging/bridging a multiple of 10	18	
Standard written method	19	
Using and applying, calculator	20	
		E2
Multiplication		
A two-digit number by a single digit	21	
By doubling and halving	22	
By 99, 100, 101, 49, 50, 51	23	
Using and applying	24	
A four-digit number by a single digit	25	
A three-digit number by a two-digit number	26	
		E3
Division		
By 2–10, including remainders	27	
Mental, beyond the tables	28	
A four-digit number by a single digit	29	
A three-digit number by a two-digit number, including remainders	30	E4
Using and applying	31	E28–29
Number properties		
Sequences	32	
Square numbers	33	
Triangular numbers investigation	34	
Products of even/odd numbers	35	
Negative numbers	36	
Divisibility by 3, 4, 6, 8	37	E5
Multiples	38	
Factors, primes	39	
Using and applying	40	E6–E7

	TEXTBOOK	EXTENSION TEXTBOOK
Fractions		
Equivalence	41–42	
Comparing and ordering	43	
Of a set/quantity, numerator $\geq$ 1	44	
Thousandths	45	
Using and applying, ratio and proportion	46	E8–E9
Decimals		
Sequences, notation	47	
Place value, comparing, ordering	48	
Rounding and approximating	49	
Mental addition	50	
Written addition	51	
Mental subtraction	52	
Written subtraction	53	
Mental multiplication, 1 decimal place	54	
Written multiplication 1/2 decimal places	55	E10–12
Mental multiplication by 10, 100, a multiple of 10	56	
Mental division by 10, 100, a single digit	57	
Written division, 1/2 decimal places	58	
Notation, sequences	59	
Place value, comparing, ordering	60	
Rounding and approximating	61	
Using and applying	62	
Percentages		
Link with fractions	63	
Of a set/quantity	64–65	
Links with fractions/decimals, comparing and ordering	66	
Using and applying	67	E30
Weight		
Reading scales to the nearest 100 g, 1/10 kg	68	
Kilogram/gram relationship	69	
The tonne	70	
Length		
Scale	71–72	
The millimetre	73	
The kilometre	74	
Choosing units	75	
Using and applying	76	
Perimeter, composite shapes	77	
Perimeter, formula	78	
Time		
24-hour times	79	
Using and applying, world times	80	
24-hour times past/to the hour, durations	81–82	
Using and applying, timetables	83	
Using and applying	84	
Reading a stopclock, minutes and seconds	85	
Using a stopwatch	86	
		E13–14

	TEXTBOOK	EXTENSION TEXTBOOK
Area		
Composite shapes	87	
Right-angled triangles	88	
Using and applying	89	
		E15
Volume/Capacity		
Centilitres, comparing and ordering	90	
Reading scales, estimating and measuring	91	
Using and applying	92	
		E16
Mixed measure		
Mixed units, using and applying	93	
Imperial/metric relationships	94–95	
2D shape		
Reflection in two lines	96	
Rotational symmetry	97	E17
Side properties	98	
Symmetry and angle properties	99	
Tangrams	100	
Circle patterns	101–102	
		E18–21
3D shape		
Nets of a cube	103	
Surface area	104	
Visualising shapes	105	
Position, movement and angle		
Co-ordinates	106	
Co-ordinates, line symmetry	107	E22
Co-ordinates, translation	108	
Co-ordinates, rotation	109	
Estimating, measuring and drawing angles	110	
Calculating angles	111	
Data handling		
Trend graphs	112	
Range, mode, median	113–114	
Mean	115	
Comparing graphs	116	
Spreadsheets	117–118	
Interpreting a database	119–120	
Bar charts with class intervals	121	
Probability	122–123	
		E23–27

1 What is the value of the **3** in each person's score?

FROGGER	Scores
Peter	94 361
Gill	135 028
Raqia	645 932

BREAKOUT	Scores
Samia	5 318 640
Dev	3 900 275
Joan	7 046 923

2 What is the value of the **red** digit in each number?

FROGGER

(a) 192 643   (b) 607 534   (c) 1 624 758

(d) 4 600 318   (e) 6 701 542   (f) 4 535 247

(g) 8 637 190   (h) 10 563 525   (i) 13 178 624

3 BREAKOUT

2 980 374	3 890 684	2 210 748	
3 980 172	3 210 650	1 809 536	1 980 374
2 809 763	4 890 395	3 809 769	

Which brick number
(a) has 210 thousands and 5 tens
(b) has 890 thousands and an odd hundreds digit
(c) is less than 2 million and has units digit 4
(d) is between 3 million and 4 million and has 7 hundreds
(e) has 809 thousands and a tens digit half of the units digit
(f) has more than 500 thousands and fewer than 3 units.

1 Rob played games against the computer.
   Who had the higher score in each game?

Game A
657 324
Rob
Computer
653 724

Game B
1 853 620
Rob
Computer
1 865 320

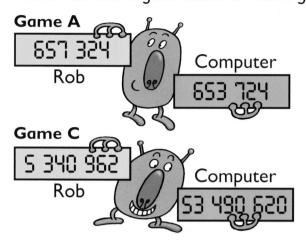

Game C
5 340 962
Rob
Computer
53 490 620

Game D
10 304 020
Rob
Computer
10 430 200

2 Which number is **(a)** highest **(b)** lowest?

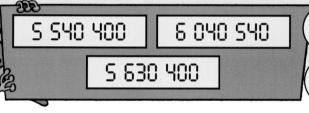

5 540 400   6 040 540

5 630 400

Five million, four hundred thousand and thirty.

Six million, fifty-four thousand three hundred.

3 List the numbers in order.
   (a) Start with the largest.

562 310   630 105   623 150   560 320   506 123

   (b) Start with the smallest.

2 754 805   745 585   745 850   7 850 450   2 458 407

4 Write the number halfway between
   (a) 3 000 000 and 4 000 000   **(b)** 1 200 000 and 1 300 000
   (c) 6 900 000 and 7 000 000   **(d)** 2 700 000 and 2 600 000.

5 Write each number using **numerals**.

   (a) Four hundred thousand, six hundred and twenty-four.

   (b) Ten million, thirty-one thousand and eighty-nine.

   (c) Seven million, six hundred and five thousand and twelve.

6 Write **in words**.
   (a)   53 000   **(b)**   175 002   **(c)**   120 713
   (d) 4 600 150   **(e)** 6 080 410   **(f)**   10 300 609

1 Find each person's total score.

	Game 1 points	Bonus or penalty points
Marvin	72 625	plus 1000
Rosie	518 300	minus 10 000
Wayne	1 400 650	plus 100 000
Kirsty	904 109	minus 100

2 Increase 3 168 035 by

(a) one thousand   (b) one hundred   (c) one hundred thousand
(d) one million   (e) ten   (f) ten thousand.

3 Decrease 1 275 463 by

(a) ten   (b) one thousand   (c) one hundred
(d) ten thousand   (e) one million   (f) one hundred thousand.

4 (a) 387 000 – 60 000   (b) 853 000 – 300 000
   (c) 6 296 500 + 500 000   (d) 7 930 200 – 7 000 000

5

Suzie   Jonas   Marie

324 000   249 000   5 470 000

How many points has
• Suzie after her score
   (a) increases by 4000   (b) **then** goes up by 50 000
• Jonas after his score
   (c) decreases by 30 000   (d) **then** goes down by 100 000
• Marie after her score
   (e) increases by 400 000   (f) **then** decreases by 2 000 000?

1 These are the points scored for zapping each type of Space Invader.

 10 points  100 points  1000 points

How many points are scored for zapping

(a) 23  (b) 23 🛸 (c) 67 🕷 (d) 67 🔺

(e) 154 🛸 (f) 209 🕷 (g) 681 🔺 (h) 356 🕷

(i) 1300 🔺 (j) 7140 🛸 (k) 2065 🕷 (l) 1001 🔺 ?

2 (a) $18 \times 10 = \blacksquare$ (b) $62 \times 100 = \blacksquare$ (c) $7 \times 1000 = \blacksquare$

(d) $1000 \times 39 = \blacksquare$ (e) $100 \times 152 = \blacksquare$ (f) $1000 \times 5260 = \blacksquare$

(g) $96 \times \blacksquare = 960$ (h) $\blacksquare \times 14 = 14\,000$ (i) $\blacksquare \times 10 = 7340$

3 Find the cost of **one** of each game.

(a) 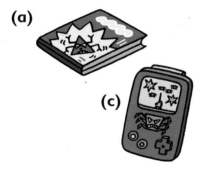 (b) (c)

Toy World Orders		
Copies bought	**Game**	**Total cost**
10		£370
100		£10 400
1000		£43 000

4 (a) $620 \div 10 = \blacksquare$ (b) $1200 \div 100 = \blacksquare$ (c) $15\,000 \div 1000 = \blacksquare$

(d) $52\,000 \div 100 = \blacksquare$ (e) $70\,000 \div 1000 = \blacksquare$ (f) $5900 \div 10 = \blacksquare$

(g) $4700 \div \blacksquare = 470$ (h) $26\,000 \div \blacksquare = 260$ (i) $\blacksquare \div 1000 = 392$

5 Find the missing numbers.

(a) 63 → ×1000 → ÷10 → ×100 → ■

(b) 51 000 → ÷100 → ÷10 → ×1000 → ■

(c) 9800 → ÷10 → ×1000 → ×10 → ■

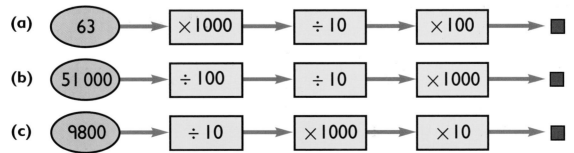

Work in a group.

Challenge Card 1

(a) About how many pennies laid side by side are in a line one metre long?

(b) Approximately how many pennies would make a line one kilometre long?

(c) What would be the approximate **value** of one kilometre of pennies?

Challenge Card 2

(a) Choose a fiction book and count the number of words on one page.

(b) Estimate the total number of words in the book.

(c) Estimate how many phone numbers are in a telephone book.

Challenge Card 3

(a) Approximately how many crayons would have a total weight of one tonne?

(b) Estimate how many mathematics textbooks together weigh one tonne.

Challenge Card 4

Over 70 years, approximately how many

(a) bowls of cereal do you think you will eat

(b) loaves of bread do you think you will eat?

1. The graph shows the number of copies of some computer games sold by *Bug Byte* in one year.

   To **the nearest thousand**, how many copies of each game were sold?

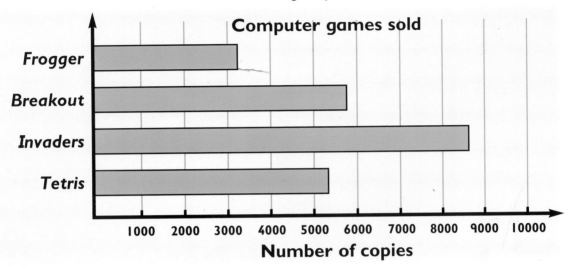

2 Round to **the nearest thousand**.

   (a) 7358   (b) 12 196   (c) 29 803   (d) 50 099
   (e) 19 583   (f) 61 758   (g) 132 052   (h) 554 454

3 Round to **the nearest hundred**.

   (a) 259   (b) 534   (c) 2688   (d) 9149
   (e) 34 769   (f) 21 081   (g) 143 208   (h) 320 851

4 This graph shows the amount of money spent **worldwide** on the games during the year.
   To **the nearest million** pounds, find the total amount spent on each game.

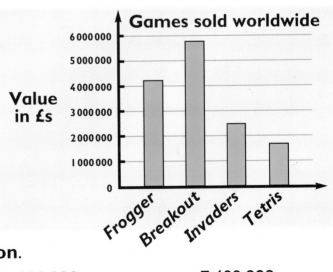

5 Round **to the nearest million**.

   (a) 3 400 000   (b) 8 888 888   (c) 7 499 999
   (d) 6 060 060   (e) 9 723 641   (f) 999 000
   (g) 11 500 001   (h) 15 055 555   (i) 19 604 072

1 Find the total of the numbers on the
   (a) circles   **(b)** squares   **(c)** hexagons   **(d)** triangles.

2 **(a)** $20 + 90 + 30 + 50$ **(b)** $80 + 40 + 20 + 80$
   (c) $60 + 30 + 40 + 70 + 50$ **(d)** $50 + 70 + 90 + 70 + 10$

3 **(a)** $36 + 19 + 24 + 11$ **(b)** $28 + 18 + 17 + 32$ **(c)** $43 + 34 + 12 + 57$
   (d) $22 + 84 + 16 + 51$ **(e)** $93 + 62 + 25$ **(f)** $84 + 43 + 69$
   (g) $76 + 53 + 30 + 14$ **(h)** $35 + 99 + 27 + 20$ **(i)** $52 + 19 + 70 + 101$
   (j) $44 + \blacksquare + 66 = 200$ **(k)** $87 + 35 + \blacksquare = 190$

4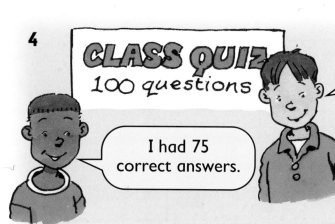

How many questions altogether did
these four children answer correctly?

5 **(a)** $62 + 63 + 61 + 60$ **(b)** $58 + 51 + 56 + 53$
   (c) $30 + 32 + 31 + 35 + 30$ **(d)** $99 + 96 + 98 + 99 + 97$

1 What is the distance between
   (a) the Start and Stage 2   **(b)** Stage 1 and Stage 3
   (c) Stage 2 and Stage 4   **(c)** Stage 3 and the Finish?

2 The Swedish car breaks down **halfway** between Stage 2 and Stage 3.
   How far is the car from   **(a)** Stage 1   **(b)** Stage 4?

3 **(a)** 664 + 326   **(b)** 353 + 427   **(c)** 739 + 142   **(d)** 575 + 307
   (e) 436 + 146   **(f)** 428 + 267   **(g)** 848 + 128   **(h)** 244 + 438
   (i) 631 + 339   **(j)** 408 + 483   **(k)** 117 + 377   **(l)** 525 + 358

4 **(a)** 149 + ■ = 682   **(b)** 519 + ■ = 756   **(c)** ■ + 216 = 491

Jarrod's Department Store
Shopper Survey

Number of shoppers entering
store between:

8.00 am – 9.00 am 190
9.00 am – 10.00 am 243
10.00 am – 11.00 am 480
11.00 am – 12.00 noon ... 374
12.00 noon – 1.00 pm 350
1.00 pm – 2.00 pm 568

1 How many shoppers entered Jarrod's between

(a) 8.00 am and 10.00 am   (b) 9.00 am and 11.00 am
(c) 10.00 am and 12.00 noon   (d) 11.00 am and 1.00 pm
(e) 12.00 noon and 2.00 pm?

2 (a) 290 + 560   (b) 464 + 470   (c) 530 + 186   (d) 663 + 263
(e) 557 + 282   (f) 182 + 685   (g) 493 + 272   (h) 275 + 341
(i) 294 + 255   (j) 381 + 166   (k) 694 + 184   (l) 177 + 732

3 (a) 193 + ■ = 753   (b) 770 + ■ = 945   (c) ■ + 453 = 909

4 The number of shoppers entering Jarrod's

- between 2.00 pm and 3.00 pm was **twice** as many
  as between 8.00 am and 9.00 am
- between 3.00 pm and 4.00 pm was **half** as many
  as between 10.00 am and 11.00 am.

How many shoppers entered Jarrod's between 2.00 pm and 4.00 pm?

Adventure Holidays

Surfing in Australia *£840*

Trekking in Nepal *£704*

Cycling in Ireland *£222*

The Holiday of a lifetime in Spain

Diving in the Caribbean *£931*

Hang-gliding in Hawaii *£955*

Canoeing in Canada *£513*

BARGAINS
BARGAINS
BARGAINS
BARGAINS

1 How much altogether do these holidays cost?

(a) Surfing and Trekking
(b) Cycling and Surfing
(c) Hang-gliding and Canoeing
(d) Trekking and Hang-gliding
(e) Diving and Surfing
(f) Canoeing and Trekking
(g) Trekking and Diving
(h) Hang-gliding and Cycling
(i) Canoeing and Diving
(j) Surfing and Canoeing

2 (a) $360 + 830$ (b) $408 + 680$ (c) $770 + 707$ (d) $154 + 924$
(e) $635 + 853$ (f) $517 + 661$ (g) $732 + 527$ (h) $444 + 814$
(i) $650 + \blacksquare = 1170$ (j) $\blacksquare + 380 = 1290$ (k) $827 + \blacksquare = 1648$

3

TRAVEL SAVE
last minute bargains!

For all Adventure Holidays
- take £29 off prices more than £600
- take £15 off prices less than £600.

Find the total **bargain price** of the Adventure Holidays.

(a) Diving and Cycling
(b) Surfing and Canoeing

Website	Number of visitors		
	Day 1	Day 2	Day 3
music4u.co	2634	2352	5637
sportsnews.co	3507	2431	4468
gameszone.co	6851	3043	2556
fashion.co	4062	1935	7043
starsigns.co	1826	5142	3737
freebie.co	5640	4255	4324

1 How many visitors altogether did each website have on

(a) Day 1 and Day 2　　　　　　(b) Day 2 and Day 3?

2 How many points in total did each **team** score playing *Firestorm*?

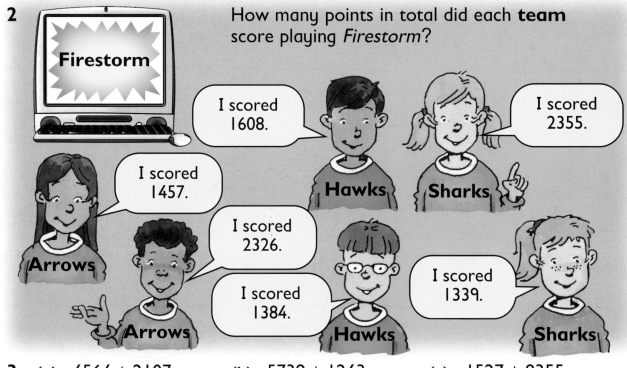

3 (a) 4564 + 2107　　(b) 5738 + 1243　　(c) 1527 + 8355

Boat Show

Swift £41 283
Gull £32 479
Puffin £23 346
Shark £5628
Marlin £6599
Dolphin £7687

1 Find the total cost of

(a) *Puffin* and *Shark* (b) *Swift* and *Marlin* (c) *Shark* and *Swift*
(d) *Gull* and *Marlin* (e) *Dolphin* and *Gull* (f) *Puffin* and *Dolphin*.

S.S. Storm   S.S. Tempest   S.S. Spray   S.S. Coral

Liner	Miles Cruised		
	Year 1	Year 2	Year 3
S.S. Storm	45 257	34 328	50 673
S.S. Tempest	28 046	33 185	46 839
S.S. Spray	15 354	27 546	35 965
S.S. Coral	45 367	44 857	49 463

2 How many miles altogether did each liner cruise in
(a) Year 1 **and** Year 2   (b) Year 2 **and** Year 3?

3 (a) 18 545 + 76 408   (b) 22 619 + 69 732   (c) 54 208 + 27 494
(d) 34 236 + 17 895   (e) 56 857 + 40 584   (f) 25 672 + 67 938

1 Find each child's total score.

Mark: 51, 8610, 429

Zoë: 6, 5924, 38

Leela: 383, 29, 3054

Sean: 8610, 66, 4, 173

Holly: 8, 3187, 6, 275

Brad: 2182, 843, 3568, 7

2 Find each team's total score.

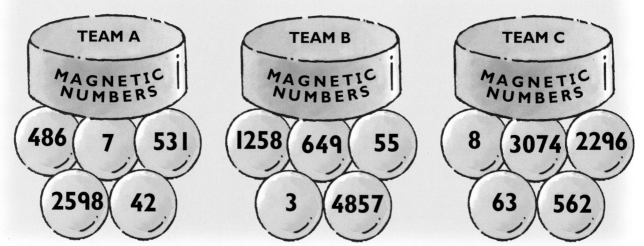

TEAM A: 486, 7, 531, 2598, 42

TEAM B: 1258, 649, 55, 3, 4857

TEAM C: 8, 3074, 2296, 63, 562

3
(a) 42 + 3509 + 8 + 176 + 55
(b) 5 + 8027 + 649 + 31 + 234
(c) 1357 + 4 + 45 + 8 + 606
(d) 1096 + 833 + 7 + 48 + 612
(e) 3 + 405 + 12 364 + 93
(f) 9 + 842 + 11 070 + 56 + 3413

4
(a) 6 + 8135 + ■ + 364 = 8600
(b) 72 + ■ + 6058 + 4 = 6240

PICK 'N' MIX

6	5754	739	13 146	82
36	3	6108	537	12 908
12 507	72	8	5956	459
210	11 365	54	9	7835
8879	893	13 077	61	5

1 **Estimate** first, then check using a calculator.

   (a) Which **row** has the greatest total?
   (b) Which **column** has the smallest total?

2 Add the numbers in five **differently-coloured** boxes each time.

   (a) What is the smallest possible total?
   (b) What is the largest possible total?

3 Which two numbers have a sum of 13 200?

4 Make a total of 999 by adding two numbers in blue boxes
   and one in a red box.

5 Choose five numbers, each from a differently-coloured box.
   Find **all** the totals that can be made by adding **four** of the numbers
   at a time.

6 Which three numbers in green boxes add to give a total
   where all of the digits are even?

1 Find the difference between the number of points scored by

   (a) the red and yellow bean bags
   (b) the green and blue bean bags
   (c) the white and orange bean bags
   (d) the black and brown bean bags.

2 **(a)** 550 − 260 = ■   **(b)** 640 − 470 = ■   **(c)** 420 − 180 = ■
   (d) 930 − 370 = ■   **(e)** 810 − 230 = ■   **(f)** 740 − 560 = ■
   (g) 730 − ■ = 380   **(h)** ■ − 540 = 290   **(i)** 860 − ■ = 570

3

260	340	480	527	613	752
Josh	Zoe	Clara	Max	Harry	Mel

Find the difference between the scores of

   (a) Max and Zoe   **(b)** Josh and Harry   **(c)** Clara and Mel
   (d) Max and Clara   **(e)** Harry and Zoe   **(f)** Mel and Josh.

4 **(a)** 324 − 160   **(b)** 936 − 580   **(c)** 875 − 690   **(d)** 705 − 420
   (e) 443 − 150   **(f)** 768 − 380   **(g)** 821 − 270   **(h)** 922 − 460
   (i) 566 − 290   **(j)** 919 − 330   **(k)** 608 − 440   **(l)** 331 − 180

5 **(a)** 736 − ■ = 556   **(b)** 951 − ■ = 261   **(c)** 611 − ■ = 281
   (d) ■ − 120 = 184   **(e)** ■ − 360 = 267   **(f)** ■ − 180 = 674

£450

£366

£187

£295

£373

£610

£560

£840

1   Find the difference between the value of

   (a)   the camera and the vase   (b)   the coin and the stamp
   (c)   the clock and the ring   (d)   the book and the sword
   (e)   the stamp and the clock   (f)   the camera and the book
   (g)   the sword and the vase   (h)   the ring and the coin.

2   (a)   820 – 442   (b)   730 – 564   (c)   550 – 178   (d)   910 – 581
    (e)   670 – 282   (f)   740 – 497   (g)   830 – 275   (h)   860 – 586
    (i)   630 – 193   (j)   650 – 464   (k)   710 – 238   (l)   940 – 679

3

243 pages

920 pages

510 pages

470 pages

  (a)   The red book has 286 pages with pictures.
       How many pages do not have pictures?

  (b)   How many more pages has the green book than the
       yellow book?

  (c)   Marvin has 127 pages of the brown book still to read.
       How many pages has he read?

  (d)   Susie has read 94 pages of the yellow book.
       Amy has read double that number of pages of the green book.
       How many pages has Amy still to read?

TRAVEL SAVE

BARGAIN BREAKS

| CYPRUS £674 | MAJORCA £345 | CRETE £591 | TURKEY £117 |
| FLORIDA £883 | IBIZA £268 | CORFU £462 | MENORCA £236 |

1　Find the difference between the cost of breaks to

(a) Crete and Ibiza　　　　(b) Cyprus and Menorca
(c) Florida and Majorca　　(d) Corfu and Turkey
(e) Menorca and Crete　　　(f) Ibiza and Florida
(g) Majorca and Cyprus　　 (h) Turkey and Majorca.

2 (a) 892 – 546　(b) 747 – 428　(c) 971 – 354　(d) 665 – 138
  (e) 995 – 759　(f) 676 – 427　(g) 781 – 563　(h) 522 – 305
  (i) 764 – 227　(j) 862 – 349　(k) 391 – 165　(l) 273 – 146

3

| **Palm Beach Hotel** 456 rooms altogether | **Coral View Hotel** 157 rooms are occupied | **Hotel Tropica** 214 rooms are vacant |

(a) *Palm Beach Hotel* has 239 rooms vacant.
How many rooms are occupied?

(b) *Coral View Hotel* has 383 rooms altogether.
How many are vacant?

(c) *Hotel Tropica* has 552 rooms altogether.
How many are occupied?

Barndale Borough Council

Village Population Survey

Village	Total population	Number of people under 25 years old
Firth	3956	703
Boulter	2894	661
Ainley	9437	2015
Sorn	7568	1352
Gilton	9985	3124
Rebway	6722	1220

1 How many people in each village are **not** under 25 years old?

2
(a) 8341 – 5031
(b) 1348 – 1036
(c) 5666 – 2222
(d) 9876 – 8765
(e) 3000 – 1001
(f) 4950 – 3145

3 The number of people aged 60 or over who live in each village is:

- Firth 538
- Boulter 745
- Ainley 3119
- Sorn 2329
- Gilton 1856
- Rebway 2607.

How many people in each village are **less than** 60 years old?

Barndale property centre

HOMES FOR SALE

two bedroom cottage

£84 375

one bedroom flat

£42 090

one bedroom apartment

£60 555

two bedroom house

£97 490

1 What is the difference between the price of

  (a) the house and the flat   **(b)** the cottage and the apartment
  (c) the flat and the cottage   **(d)** the house and the cottage
  (e) the apartment and the flat   **(f)** the apartment and the house?

2 **(a)** 34 672 − 19 549   **(b)** 47 563 − 27 738   **(c)** 75 282 − 49 367
    (d) 56 784 − 32 995   **(e)** 23 504 − 14 619   **(f)** 90 000 − 53 426

3

Mowbray Mansion
Price in 1910: £4525
Current Price: £754 990

What is the difference between the 1910 price and
the current price of Mowbray Mansion?

4 **(a)** 23 756 − 83   **(b)** 42 195 − 3047   **(c)** 835 912 − 6208
    (d) 306 974 − 988   **(e)** 51 234 − 698   **(f)** 237 819 − 8939
    (g) 643 215 − 76   **(h)** 903 070 − 1264   **(i)** 1 000 000 − 5962

1 The difference between two multiples of 10 is 330.
Their total is 710.
What are the two numbers?

2 Copy and complete each subtraction chain.

(a) 8000 − 2700 → ■ − 1500 → ■ − 2250 → ■ − 600 → ■ − 384 → ■

(b) 6000 − 3524 → ■ − 1258 → ■ − 400 → ■ − 209 → ■ − 440 → ■

3

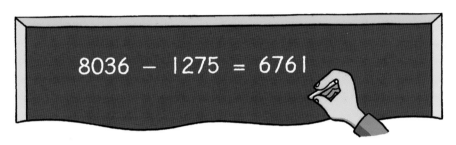

8036 − 1275 = 6761

Use the subtraction story to find:

(a) 8036 − 6760   (b) 6761 + 1271   (c) 8000 − 6761
(d) 1280 + 6761   (e) 8036 − 1250   (f) 8030 − 1270

4 List pairs of these numbers which have a difference of 79.

61   132   290   177   211
256   359   108

5   Find the missing numbers.

(a) 803 516 − ■ = 783 929   (b) ■ − 15 889 = 77 777

6 Find the missing digits.

(a) 67■5 − △306 = 1409   (b) 93 26■ − 4△◇51 = 46 014

| Happytot £24 | Robotot £33 | Furrytot £27 | Nosytot £46 |

1 Find the cost of

  (a) 4 Happytots   **(b)** 2 Furrytots   **(c)** 6 Nosytots

  (d) 3 Robotots   **(e)** 5 Happytots   **(f)** 3 Furrytots

  (g) 8 Nosytots   **(h)** 7 Furrytots   **(i)** 5 Robotots

2 **(a)** 3×29 **(b)** 2×67 **(c)** 76×5 **(d)** 89×4

    (e) 6×38 **(f)** 46×7 **(g)** 65×8 **(h)** 9×18

3

| 4 Happytots | 6 Furrytots | 8 Robotots |

How many

  (a) Happytots are in 45 boxes   **(b)** Furrytots are in 27 boxes

  (c) Robotots are in 68 boxes   **(d)** Happytots are in 76 boxes

  (e) Furrytots are in 34 boxes   **(f)** Robotots are in 69 boxes?

4 Seven children each have a complete collection of 36 Cybertots. How many Cybertots do they have altogether?

5 A battery pack for a Cybertot costs £9. What is the cost of 53 battery packs?

1 (a) 5×34 (b) 62×5 (c) 35×18 (d) 16×45
(e) 35×14 (f) 54×5 (g) 14×25 (h) 25×16

2 (a) Multiply 5 by 44. (b) 18 times 45
(c) 5 multiplied by 76 (d) Multiply 14 by 15.

3 How many sheets are there in

(a) 12 notepads (b) 18 notepads?

15 sheets

4 How many pencils are there in

(a) 35 packets (b) 45 packets?

12 pencils

5 (a) 16×13 (b) 18×17 (c) 14×33 (d) 12×37
(e) 27×14 (f) 44×12 (g) 31×16 (h) 18×42

6 How many

(a) books are in 12 boxes
(b) comics are in 18 boxes?

22 books

29 comics

7 (a) 50×26 (b) 50×38 (c) 42×50 (d) 54×50
(e) 25×24 (f) 25×36 (g) 48×25 (h) 56×25

8 Which pair of numbers gives
a product of

(a) 800 (b) 1300?

| 25 | 26 | 32 | 50 | 52 |

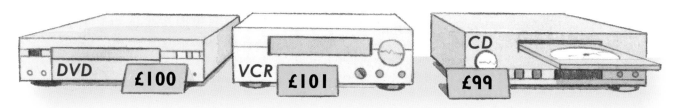

1 How much does it cost to buy

(a) • 14 DVD players   • 14 VCRs   • 14 CD players

(b) • 23 DVD players   • 23 VCRs   • 23 CD players?

2
(a) 100×34 (b) 101×17 (c) 99×16

(d) 101×28 (e) 100×19 (f) 101×31

(g) 99×34 (h) 100×26 (i) 99×28

3

£50   £51   £49

(a) Find the cost of

    • 13 blue radios   • 13 green radios   • 13 red radios

(b) Repeat to find the cost of 24 radios in each colour.

(c) Repeat for 19 radios.

4
(a) 50×18 (b) 51×12 (c) 49×26

(d) 49×17 (e) 50×21 (f) 51×27

5 What is the total cost of

(a) 49 mobile phones

(b) 50 headphones

(c) 46 games

(d) 49 headphones

(e) 51 mobile phones

(f) 29 minidisc players?

£27   £38   £99   £101

Bostock Ballet

	Grand Circle	Front Stalls	Back Stalls
Adult	£28	£23	£15
Child	£21	£17	£12

1 How much does it cost to buy

(a) 7 adult tickets in the Grand Circle
(b) 9 child tickets in the Front Stalls
(c) 14 adult tickets in the Back Stalls
(d) 6 adult tickets and 4 child tickets in the Front Stalls
(e) 8 adult tickets and 5 child tickets in the Grand Circle
(f) 12 adult tickets and 24 child tickets in the Back Stalls?

2 Blythwood School orders 58 child tickets and 7 adult tickets for the Wednesday matinee.

How much does this cost altogether?

Bostock Ballet
Wednesday matinee
All seats
Adult £13 Child £6

3

	Grand Circle	Back Stalls	Front Stalls
Number of rows	13	34	17
Number of seats in a row	50	49	51

How many seats are there in the

(a) Grand Circle   (b) Front Stalls   (c) Back Stalls?

4 These items were sold during an interval.

 18 45 p    14 32 p    49 58p    25 27 p

How much was spent altogether?

Travelsave
Luxury Holidays

Egypt	Australia	Mexico	Kenya

adult £2517	adult £7018	adult £4356	adult £2976
child £1259	child £3509	child £2178	child £1488

China	Alaska	India	Brazil

adult £5568	adult £7466	adult £5472	adult £9630
child £2784	child £3733	child £2736	child £4815

1 Find the total cost of each holiday.

- **(a)** 7 adults to Kenya
- **(b)** 3 adults to Australia
- **(c)** 5 adults to Mexico
- **(d)** 2 adults to Egypt
- **(e)** 9 adults to India
- **(f)** 6 adults to Alaska
- **(g)** 4 adults to China
- **(h)** 8 adults to Brazil

2 Find the total cost of each holiday.

- **(a)** 2 adults and 5 children to India
- **(b)** 3 adults and 7 children to Brazil
- **(c)** 4 adults and 8 children to Australia
- **(d)** 6 adults and 9 children to Kenya

3

The Blake family won a luxury holiday. The value of the holiday was £19 152. Which country did they visit?

Each picture shows:
- the plane's destination
- the number of passengers it can carry.

Majorca   236

Ibiza   275

Malta 78

Rhodes   323

Tenerife   368

Corfu   251

Turkey   294

Cyprus   342

All HE flights are full.

1 Find the total number of each people carried to each destination.

(a) 42 flights to Malta
(b) 28 flights to Ibiza
(c) 53 flights to Majorca
(d) 27 flights to Tenerife
(e) 29 flights to Rhodes
(f) 18 flights to Cyprus
(g) 37 flights to Corfu
(h) 33 flights to Turkey

2 A ticket for a flight to Malta costs £127.

What is the total amount collected for one flight?

3 On flights to Cyprus each passenger can take 23 kg of luggage.

Find the total weight of luggage on one flight.

4 Headphones are handed out on flights to Tenerife and Corfu.

How many headphones are handed out on

(a) 38 Tenerife flights
(b) 63 Corfu flights?

1 Divide equally.

   (a) 42 mountain bikes ⟶ 6 racks   **(b)** 48 skateboards ⟶ 8 boxes
   (c) 40 basketballs ⟶ 8 nets   **(d)** 81 golf clubs ⟶ 9 bags
   (e) 50 rollerblades ⟶ 10 cases   **(f)** 28 snooker cues ⟶ 7 tables

2 **(a)** $49 \div 7$ **(b)** $40 \div 4$ **(c)** $70 \div 7$ **(d)** $45 \div 9$ **(e)** $56 \div 8$ **(f)** $54 \div 6$
    (g) $72 \div 8$ **(h)** $27 \div 9$ **(i)** $36 \div 9$ **(j)** $35 \div 7$ **(k)** $100 \div 10$ **(l)** $63 \div 7$

3 Find the missing numbers.

  (a) $\dfrac{21}{\blacksquare} = 7$ **(b)** $\dfrac{\blacksquare}{9} = 8$ **(c)** $\dfrac{30}{\blacksquare} = 5$ **(d)** $\dfrac{\blacksquare}{6} = 8$ **(e)** $\dfrac{60}{\blacksquare} = 10$

  (f) $\dfrac{\blacksquare}{8} = 4$ **(g)** $\dfrac{24}{\blacksquare} = 3$ **(h)** $\dfrac{\blacksquare}{4} = 4$ **(i)** $\dfrac{36}{\blacksquare} = 6$ **(j)** $\dfrac{\blacksquare}{10} = 9$

4 Divide the equipment equally among the teams.
   How many items are given to each team and how many are left over?

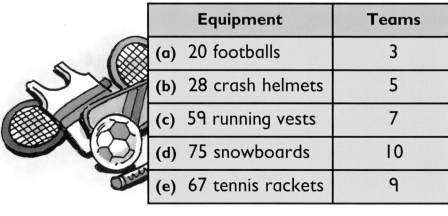

Equipment	Teams
(a) 20 footballs	3
(b) 28 crash helmets	5
(c) 59 running vests	7
(d) 75 snowboards	10
(e) 67 tennis rackets	9

5 **(a)** $80 \div 9 = \blacksquare$ **(b)** $47 \div 7 = \blacksquare$ **(c)** $86 \div 10 = \blacksquare$ **(d)** $19 \div 2 = \blacksquare$
    (e) $45 \div 6 = \blacksquare$ **(f)** $29 \div 9 = \blacksquare$ **(g)** $53 \div 5 = \blacksquare$ **(h)** $7 \div 8 = \blacksquare$
    (i) $\frac{1}{6}$ of $62 = \blacksquare$ **(j)** $\frac{1}{3}$ of $26 = \blacksquare$ **(k)** $\frac{1}{8}$ of $86 = \blacksquare$ **(l)** $\frac{1}{7}$ of $20 = \blacksquare$

6 One eighth of the practice golf balls are *Superflite*.
   One seventh of the rest are *Fairway*.
   How many golf balls are **not** *Superflite*
   or *Fairway*?

64 golf balls

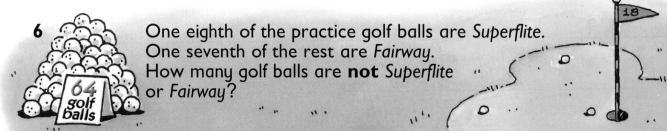

ASHWAY LEISURE CENTRE
Sponsored Sports Week

1 The players in each team raised an equal amount of money.

We raised a total of two hundred and forty pounds.

We raised six hundred and thirty pounds altogether.

Our total was eight hundred and ten pounds.

How much money was raised by each player in

(a) the red team (b) the blue team (c) the green team?

2
(a) $320 \div 8 = \blacksquare$ (b) $480 \div 6 = \blacksquare$ (c) $270 \div 3 = \blacksquare$ (d) $540 \div 9 = \blacksquare$
(e) $360 \div 4 = \blacksquare$ (f) $450 \div 5 = \blacksquare$ (g) $490 \div 7 = \blacksquare$ (h) $560 \div 8 = \blacksquare$
(i) $280 \div \blacksquare = 40$ (j) $720 \div \blacksquare = 80$ (k) $640 \div \blacksquare = 80$ (l) $210 \div \blacksquare = 70$

3 The cyclists in each team completed an equal number of laps. How many laps did each cycle?

(a) Team total: 78 laps (b) Team total: 108 laps (c) Team total: 105 laps (d) Team total: 104 laps

4
(a) $52 \div 4$ (b) $91 \div 7$ (c) $60 \div 5$ (d) $39 \div 3$ (e) $99 \div 9$ (f) $84 \div 6$
(g) $96 \div 8$ (h) $57 \div 3$ (i) $72 \div 6$ (j) $68 \div 4$ (k) $75 \div 5$ (l) $117 \div 9$

5
(a) $848 \div 4$ (b) $763 \div 7$ (c) $819 \div 9$ (d) $486 \div 6$ (e) $159 \div 3$
(f) $455 \div 5$ (g) $832 \div 8$ (h) $567 \div 7$ (i) $624 \div 6$ (j) $404 \div 4$

1 Joe Bloggs' election publicity items are shared equally among boxes. How many items are in each box?

(a)	(b)	(c)	(d)	(e)
4260 stickers	2892 badges	3672 posters	5724 leaflets	7032 letters

in 5 boxes	in 3 boxes	in 9 boxes	in 6 boxes	in 8 boxes

2 (a) $6252 \div 4$ (b) $7945 \div 7$ (c) $8758 \div 2$ (d) $9837 \div 9$
(e) $9132 \div 6$ (f) $8256 \div 4$ (g) $9072 \div 7$ (h) $7005 \div 5$

3 Voting papers are shared equally among vote counters. How many papers does each counter receive and how many are left over?

(a)	(b)	(c)
5027 voting papers	**3853** voting papers	**2200** voting papers
6 counters	8 counters	3 counters

4 (a) $3575 \div 4$ (b) $1986 \div 5$ (c) $4903 \div 3$ (d) $3157 \div 2$
(e) $9041 \div 7$ (f) $8200 \div 8$ (g) $9119 \div 9$ (h) $6006 \div 5$

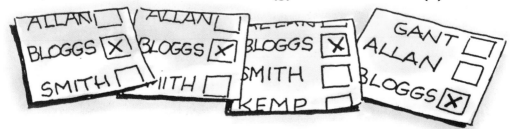

1 Emergency sacks of food are divided equally among crates.
How many sacks are in each crate?

(a) 552 sacks of beans in 24 crates.

(b) 875 sacks of grain in 35 crates.

(c) 992 sacks of rice in 31 crates.

(d) 806 sacks of flour in 26 crates.

2 (a) 770 ÷ 22   **(b)** 962 ÷ 37   **(c)** 986 ÷ 29   **(d)** 644 ÷ 14

3 Medical items are shared equally among boxes.
How many items are in each box and how many are left over?

| 312 bandages | 684 blankets | 676 syringes |
| in 16 boxes | in 27 boxes | in 19 boxes |

4 (a) 987 ÷ 41   **(b)** 970 ÷ 23   **(c)** 686 ÷ 15   **(d)** 898 ÷ 28
   (e) 783 ÷ 18   **(f)** 996 ÷ 32   **(g)** 891 ÷ 21   **(h)** 696 ÷ 17

Zipways Security

1 The badges show each security guard's number.

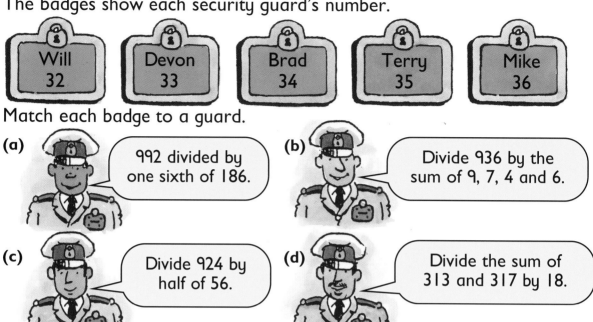

| Will 32 | Devon 33 | Brad 34 | Terry 35 | Mike 36 |

Match each badge to a guard.

(a) 992 divided by one sixth of 186.

(b) Divide 936 by the sum of 9, 7, 4 and 6.

(c) Divide 924 by half of 56.

(d) Divide the sum of 313 and 317 by 18.

2 Write a division clue for the remaining security guard's badge number.

3

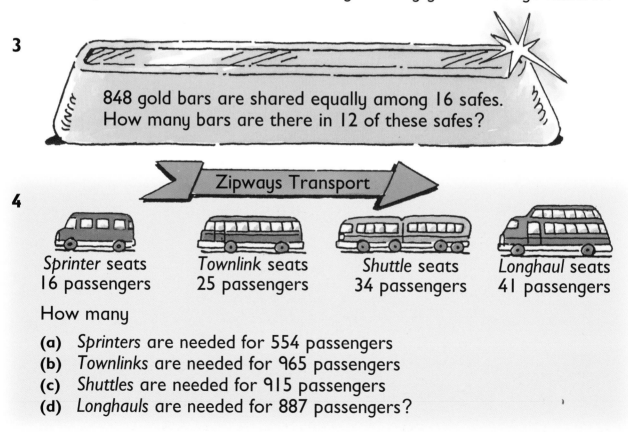

848 gold bars are shared equally among 16 safes. How many bars are there in 12 of these safes?

Zipways Transport

4

Sprinter seats 16 passengers

Townlink seats 25 passengers

Shuttle seats 34 passengers

Longhaul seats 41 passengers

How many

(a) *Sprinters* are needed for 554 passengers

(b) *Townlinks* are needed for 965 passengers

(c) *Shuttles* are needed for 915 passengers

(d) *Longhauls* are needed for 887 passengers?

5 Each *Zipways* plane has seats for 32 passengers.
How many planes would be needed to carry 760 passengers?

TOPIC ASSESSMENT

1 Write each child's number sequence.

(a)
Start at 24. Count on in 6s to 96.

(b)
Start at 3. Count on in 8s to 67.

(c)
Start at 72. Count back in 7s to 9.

(d)
Start at 94. Count back in 11s to 6.

(e)
Start at 42. Count on in 9s to 96.

(f)
Start at 257. Count back in 25s to 7.

2
128, 64, 32, 16, 8, 4, 2, 1

The rule for my number sequence is **divide by 2** each time.

Copy each sequence and write the next four numbers.
Write the rule for each sequence.

(a) 10, 25, 40, 55, ...
(b) 5, 12, 19, 26, ...
(c) 79, 73, 67, 61, ...
(d) 263, 242, 221, 200, ...
(e) 25, 44, 63, 82, ...
(f) 92, 84, 76, 68, ...
(g) 10, 9·5, 9, 8·5, ...
(h) ⁻9, ⁻6, ⁻3, 0, ...
(i) 27, 18, 9, 0, ...
(j) 1, 2, 4, 8, ...

3 Copy and complete each number sequence and write the rule.

(a) 5, 16, 27, ■, ■, 60
(b) 79, 64, 49, ■, ■, 4
(c) 13, 38, 63, ■, ■, 138
(d) 122, ■, ■, 65, 46, 27
(e) 21, 10, ■, ■, ⁻23, ⁻34
(f) 36, 15, ■, ⁻27, ⁻48, ■
(g) ■, 31, 50, ■, 88, 107
(h) 3, 6, 12, 24, ■, ■

1 Which of the door numbers are

   (a) square numbers

   (b) square **and** even

   (c) odd **and not** square?

2 **(a)** List the first twelve square numbers.

   (b) Calculate each square number from 13^2 to 20^2.

3 Use your answers to question **2.**

   (a) Find a pair of square numbers with a total of ● 65   ● 250.

   (b) Find pairs of square numbers with a total which is also
      a square number.

4

Bill the builder lays **square** patios using identical square slabs.

   (a) How many slabs lie along each edge of a patio with

      ● 25 slabs   ● 81 slabs ?

   (b) Find the number of slabs on each edge of a patio with

      ● 961 slabs   ● 2704 slabs.

5 **(a)** Copy this pattern and extend
      it for two more rows.

$$2^2 - 1^2 = 4 - 1 = 3 = 2 + 1$$
$$3^2 - 2^2 = 9 - 4 = 5 = 3 + 2$$
$$4^2 - 3^2 = 16 - 9 = 7 = 4 + 3$$

   (b) **Without** extending the pattern further, find mentally

      ● $9^2 - 8^2$ ● $10^2 - 9^2$

   (c) Copy and complete Bill's rule.

> The difference between the squares of two
> consecutive whole numbers is equal to ...

1 Stanley arranges displays of items for sale in a supermarket.

(a) How many boxes are in each of these four stacks?

(b) Draw the fifth and sixth stacks in Stanley's pattern. How many boxes are in each stack?

(c) **Without** drawing stacks write the number of boxes in the seventh and eighth stacks.

(d) How can you calculate the number of boxes in the ninth stack?

(e) The stacks of boxes are triangular shaped. The numbers 1, 3, 6, 10, ... and so on are called **triangular numbers.**

List the triangular numbers from 1 to 120.

2 (a) Stanley puts his second and third stacks together like this: Draw pairs of consecutive stacks put together in the same way.

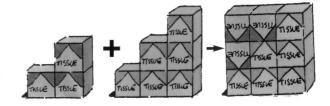

(b) Add pairs of consecutive triangular numbers. What type of number is each total?

3 (a) Which triangular numbers less than 100 are also square numbers?

(b) Make 100 by adding
   • two triangular numbers   • three triangular numbers.

1 (a) Grandpa's age is an even number **between** 50 and 60. What age could he be?

(b) Jenny's age is an odd number between 5 and 15. What age could she be?

2

Find the product of the numbers on these birthday badges.

(a) red and blue
(b) yellow and green
(c) orange and purple
(d) orange and yellow
(e) red and purple
(f) green and blue

3 (a) In question **2**, what type of number is • each badge number
• each product?

(b) What is true about the product of two even numbers?

4 Find the product of the numbers on each pair of birthday cards.

(a) **(b)** **(c)**

(d) **(e)** **(f)**

5 What is true about the product of two odd numbers?

6 Investigation Find out about the product of an odd and an even number. Write about what you find.

1 Write these temperatures in order.
- Start with the **lowest**.
  - **(a)** 6°C, ⁻2°C, 10°C, ⁻5°C, ⁻10°C
  - **(b)** ⁻4°C, 7°C, 0°C, ⁻8°C, 3°C
- Start with the **highest**.
  - **(c)** ⁻27°C, 1°C, 26°C, ⁻1°C, ⁻14°C
  - **(d)** ⁻34°C, ⁻2°C, 2°C, ⁻43°C, 24°C

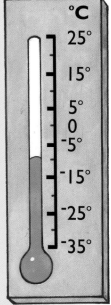

2 **(a)** What temperature is shown by the thermometer?
(b) What will the temperature be after it falls by 15 degrees?

3 What is the new temperature after a temperature of 6°C
- **(a)** rises by 7 degrees
- **(b)** falls by 4 degrees
- **(c)** falls by 6 degrees
- **(d)** falls by 26 degrees?

4 What is the new temperature after a temperature of ⁻11°C
- **(a)** falls by 3 degrees
- **(b)** rises by 3 degrees
- **(c)** falls by 11 degrees
- **(d)** rises by 22 degrees?

5 Find, in degrees, the difference between temperatures of
(a) 16°C and ⁻2°C   **(b)** 4°C and ⁻32°C   **(c)** ⁻5°C and ⁻35°C.

6 The normal water level in a swimming pool should be 2 metres.
Sally keeps a record of the water level, **in centimetres,** above or below normal like this:

Mon	Tue	Wed	Thu	Fri	Sat
+4	+2	⁻3	⁻5	0	⁻4

Write the water level for each day.

7 **(a)** List all the different pairs of whole numbers which have a total of 6.
(b) Find pairs of numbers, **one of which is negative**, which total 6.

5 + 1 = 6
4 + 2 = 6
3 +

1 (a) **Without dividing**, list the runners' numbers which are exactly divisible by 4.

   (b) Explain how you found the numbers.

2 (a) Which of the runners' numbers are exactly divisible by 8?

   (b) Copy and complete.

Numbers exactly divisible by 8	168						
Half of the number	84						
Is the half exactly divisible by 4?	Yes						

   (c) How can you tell, without dividing, that a number is exactly divisible by 8?

3

96	246	303	67	648	810	951

293	534	174	429	342	1668	785

   (a) **Without dividing**, list the vest numbers which are exactly divisible by 3.

   (b) Explain how you found the numbers.

4 (a) List the vest numbers which are exactly divisible by 6.

   (b) Check, without dividing, that what Rosa says about these numbers is true.

   > Each number is even...
   > ...and is exactly divisible by 3.

   (c) How can you tell, without dividing, that a number is exactly divisible by 6?

5 Without dividing, list the numbers from 430 to 440 which are

   (a) exactly divisible by 8   (b) **not** exactly divisible by 6.

1 List the table numbers which are • multiples of 4 • multiples of 5.

2 **(a)** List the first ten • multiples of 7 • multiples of 9.
 (b) Which multiples of 7 in part **(a)** are exactly divisible by 3?
 (c) Which multiples of 9 in part **(a)** are exactly divisible by 4?

3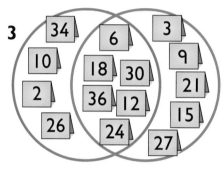

 (a) What type of numbers are in
 • the red circle • the green circle?
 (b) List, in order, the numbers that are in **both**
 the red **and** the green circles.
 (c) Describe these numbers in **two** different ways.

4 **(a)** List the first twenty • multiples of 2 • multiples of 5.
 (b) List the numbers in part **(a)** that are multiples of **both** 2 **and** 5.
 (c) Which is the smallest number that is a **common** multiple of 2 and 5?

5 Write the smallest number that is a common multiple of
 (a) 2 and 7 **(b)** 6 and 5 **(c)** 3 and 8 **(d)** 7 and 5
 (e) 4 and 10 **(f)** 12 and 8 **(g)** 6 and 15 **(h)** 9 and 36

6 **(a)** What colour is the 60th square in this pattern?

 ▢ ▢ ▢ ▢ ▢ ▢ ▢ ▢ ▢ ▢ ▢ ▢ ▢ ▢ ▢ ▢ ▢ ▢ ▢ ...

 (b) What is the position in the pattern of the 22nd yellow square?

7 **(a)** What colour is the 67th square in this pattern?

 ▢ ▢ ▢ ▢ ▢ ▢ ▢ ▢ ▢ ▢ ▢ ▢ ▢ ▢ ...

 (b) What is the position of the 18th orange square?

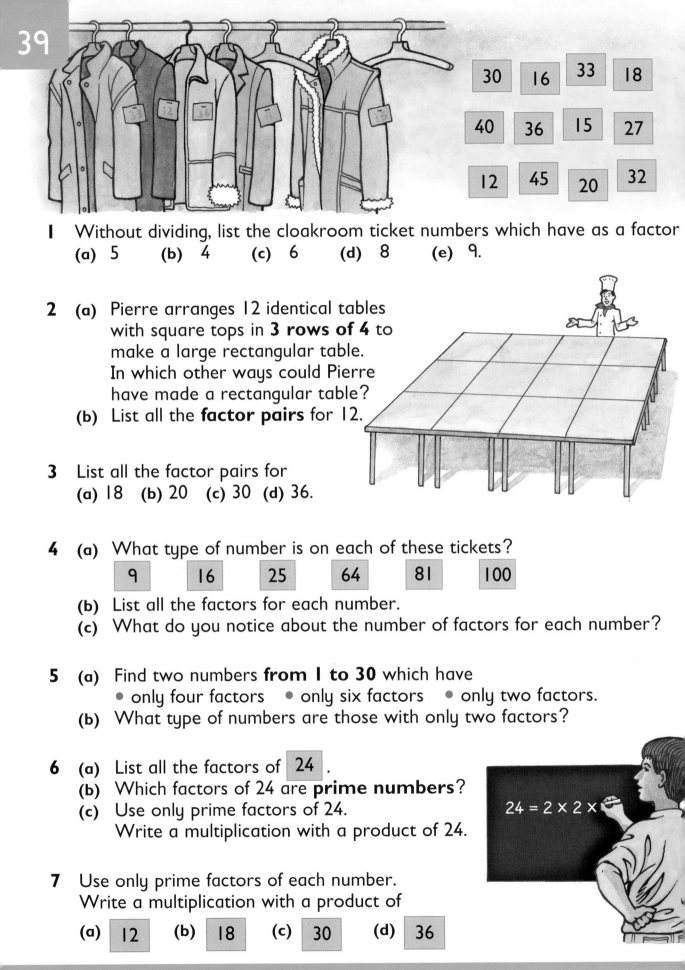

30	16	33	18
40	36	15	27
12	45	20	32

1 Without dividing, list the cloakroom ticket numbers which have as a factor
(a) 5   (b) 4   (c) 6   (d) 8   (e) 9.

2 (a) Pierre arranges 12 identical tables
with square tops in **3 rows of 4** to
make a large rectangular table.
In which other ways could Pierre
have made a rectangular table?
(b) List all the **factor pairs** for 12.

3 List all the factor pairs for
(a) 18   (b) 20   (c) 30   (d) 36.

4 (a) What type of number is on each of these tickets?

| 9 | 16 | 25 | 64 | 81 | 100 |

(b) List all the factors for each number.
(c) What do you notice about the number of factors for each number?

5 (a) Find two numbers **from 1 to 30** which have
   • only four factors   • only six factors   • only two factors.
(b) What type of numbers are those with only two factors?

6 (a) List all the factors of 24 .
(b) Which factors of 24 are **prime numbers**?
(c) Use only prime factors of 24.
Write a multiplication with a product of 24.

24 = 2 × 2 ×

7 Use only prime factors of each number.
Write a multiplication with a product of
(a) 12   (b) 18   (c) 30   (d) 36

Captain Nero
Lock - Keeper's Cottage
Canal Bank
Newkirk
NK66GY

1 Write True or False for each statement about the **number** from Captain Nero's postcode.

(a) The number is even.
(b) It is a multiple of 5.
(c) It is a common multiple of 6 and 11.
(d) One of its factors is 7.
(e) One of its factor pairs is 2 and 33.
(f) It is a square number.
(g) It is a triangular number.

2 Match each person to the number from their postcode.

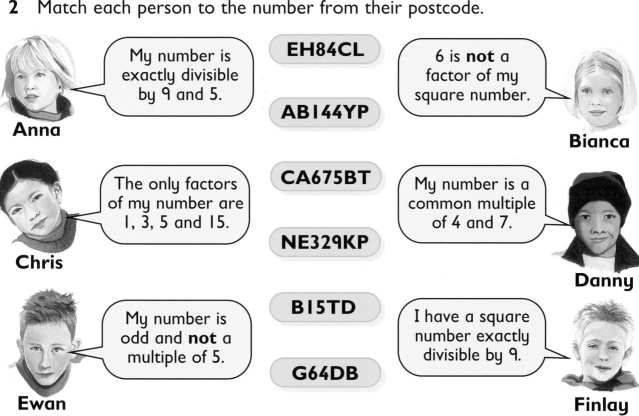

Anna: My number is exactly divisible by 9 and 5.

EH84CL

AB144YP

Bianca: 6 is **not** a factor of my square number.

Chris: The only factors of my number are 1, 3, 5 and 15.

CA675BT

NE329KP

Danny: My number is a common multiple of 4 and 7.

Ewan: My number is odd and **not** a multiple of 5.

B15TD

G64DB

Finlay: I have a square number exactly divisible by 9.

3 Describe the number from each of these postcodes in as many different ways as you can.

(a) HX81CF
(b) PH45GZ
(c) LA216MA

1 Write the equal fractions story for each pair of shapes.

(a)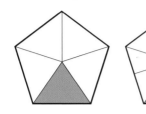

(b)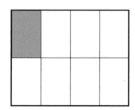

(c)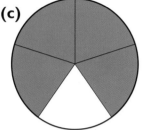

(d)

(e)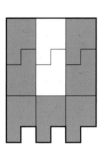

(f)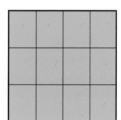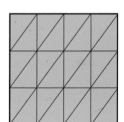

2 Copy and complete.

(a) $\frac{1}{2} = \frac{}{10}$

(b) $\frac{1}{5} = \frac{}{20}$

(c) $\frac{1}{10} = \frac{}{100}$

(d) $\frac{1}{7} = \frac{}{21}$

(e) $\frac{}{12} = \frac{3}{4}$

(f) $\frac{}{15} = \frac{2}{3}$

(g) $\frac{}{14} = \frac{2}{7}$

(h) $\frac{}{90} = \frac{4}{9}$

(i) $\frac{3}{6} = \frac{}{30}$

(j) $\frac{}{56} = \frac{6}{8}$

(k) $\frac{5}{10} = \frac{}{100}$

(l) $\frac{}{80} = \frac{3}{4}$

3 Change

(a) $\frac{1}{3}$ to sixths

(b) $\frac{1}{9}$ to eighteenths

(c) $\frac{7}{8}$ to eightieths

(d) $\frac{9}{10}$ to hundredths

(e) $\frac{4}{6}$ to thirty-sixths

(f) $\frac{4}{10}$ to fortieths.

4 Write **three** other fractions equal to

(a) $\frac{1}{4}$

(b) $\frac{3}{5}$

(c) $\frac{4}{7}$

(d) $\frac{3}{3}$

1 Copy and complete.

(a) $\frac{3}{6} = \frac{}{2}$ (b) $\frac{2}{12} = \frac{}{6}$ (c) $\frac{6}{15} = \frac{}{5}$ (d) $\frac{8}{12} = \frac{}{3}$

(e) $\frac{}{7} = \frac{30}{35}$ (f) $\frac{}{9} = \frac{24}{27}$ (g) $\frac{}{4} = \frac{15}{20}$ (h) $\frac{}{10} = \frac{60}{100}$

(i) $\frac{24}{48} = \frac{}{8}$ (j) $\frac{}{4} = \frac{25}{100}$ (k) $\frac{40}{50} = \frac{}{5}$ (l) $\frac{}{9} = \frac{48}{72}$

2 Change

(a) $\frac{12}{18}$ to thirds   (b) $\frac{15}{40}$ to eighths   (c) $\frac{75}{100}$ to quarters

(d) $\frac{16}{20}$ to tenths   (e) $\frac{12}{36}$ to ninths   (f) $\frac{14}{49}$ to sevenths.

3 Which of these fractions are equal to   (a) $\frac{2}{3}$ (b) $\frac{3}{4}$ (c) $\frac{4}{5}$?

| $\frac{80}{100}$ | $\frac{60}{80}$ | $\frac{20}{30}$ | $\frac{33}{40}$ | $\frac{20}{25}$ | $\frac{21}{28}$ | $\frac{36}{45}$ | $\frac{25}{35}$ | $\frac{16}{24}$ |

4 Simplify.

(a) $\frac{8}{16}$ (b) $\frac{6}{18}$ (c) $\frac{35}{50}$ (d) $\frac{15}{24}$ (e) $\frac{45}{81}$

(f) $\frac{30}{90}$ (g) $\frac{12}{84}$ (h) $\frac{28}{70}$ (i) $\frac{75}{90}$ (j) $\frac{84}{96}$

5 Ayub and Bea played 30 games of Noughts and Crosses. Ayub won 10 games, Bea won 6 games and the rest were draws.

What **fraction** of the games
(a) were won by Bea
(b) were won by Ayub
(c) were draws?

6 The table shows the results when Bea threw two dice 50 times.

What **fraction** of the throws resulted in
(a) an odd and an even number
(b) two odd numbers
(c) two even numbers?

Numbers on dice	Frequency
1 odd + 1 even	25
2 odd	10
2 even	15

One tenth is smaller than one fifth.

One quarter is greater than one sixth.

1 Write > or < between each pair of fractions.

(a) $\frac{1}{3}$ and $\frac{1}{2}$ (b) $\frac{1}{6}$ and $\frac{1}{7}$ (c) $\frac{1}{12}$ and $\frac{1}{15}$ (d) $\frac{1}{20}$ and $\frac{1}{19}$

2 Write **three** fractions

(a) greater than one sixth   (b) smaller than one third.

3 Copy and complete.

(a) $\frac{1}{10}$ is ___ of $\frac{1}{5}$

$\frac{1}{5}$ is ___ $\frac{1}{10}$

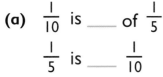

$\frac{1}{6}$ is half of $\frac{1}{3}$

$\frac{1}{3}$ is twice $\frac{1}{6}$

(b) $\frac{1}{20}$ is ___ of $\frac{1}{10}$

$\frac{1}{10}$ is ___ $\frac{1}{20}$

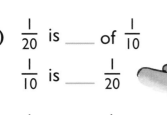

(c) $\frac{1}{8}$ is ___ $\frac{1}{16}$ (d) $\frac{1}{2}$ is ___ times $\frac{1}{6}$ (e) $\frac{1}{10}$ is ___ times $\frac{1}{100}$

$\frac{1}{16}$ is ___ of $\frac{1}{8}$ $\frac{1}{6}$ is ___ of $\frac{1}{2}$ $\frac{1}{100}$ is ___ of $\frac{1}{10}$

4 List the numbers in order.

(a) Start with the smallest.   (b) Start with the largest.

$1\frac{1}{12}$ $2\frac{1}{3}$ $1\frac{2}{3}$ $2\frac{7}{12}$ $1\frac{1}{2}$ $2\frac{3}{5}$ $3\frac{3}{10}$ $2\frac{9}{10}$ $2\frac{3}{4}$ $3\frac{1}{2}$

5 Copy this part of a number line which has 30 divisions.

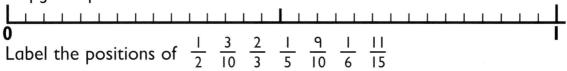

0

Label the positions of $\frac{1}{2}$ $\frac{3}{10}$ $\frac{2}{3}$ $\frac{1}{5}$ $\frac{9}{10}$ $\frac{1}{6}$ $\frac{11}{15}$

6 Write the number halfway between

(a) $\frac{3}{5}$ and $\frac{4}{5}$ (b) $\frac{1}{3}$ and $\frac{2}{3}$ (c) $3\frac{1}{4}$ and $3\frac{1}{2}$ (d) $4\frac{1}{2}$ and $4\frac{5}{8}$

7 Find a fraction

(a) greater than $\frac{1}{2}$ and less than $\frac{3}{5}$ (b) less than $\frac{1}{3}$ and greater than $\frac{1}{4}$

30 first class

36 second class

1 Find each fraction of the first class stamps.

(a) $\frac{1}{2}$ (b) $\frac{1}{5}$ (c) $\frac{2}{5}$ (d) $\frac{1}{6}$ (e) $\frac{5}{6}$ (f) $\frac{2}{3}$

2 Find each fraction of the second class stamps.

(a) $\frac{3}{4}$ (b) $\frac{1}{9}$ (c) $\frac{7}{9}$ (d) $\frac{1}{6}$ (e) $\frac{3}{6}$ (f) $\frac{2}{3}$

3 (a) $\frac{1}{100}$ of 600   (b) $\frac{3}{10}$ of 70   (c) $\frac{4}{5}$ of 45   (d) two thirds of 21

   (e) $\frac{1}{7}$ of 56   (f) $\frac{3}{8}$ of 48   (g) $\frac{5}{6}$ of 42   (h) two ninths of 72

4 (a) $\frac{1}{4}$ of 80   (b) $\frac{3}{5}$ of 55   (c) $\frac{7}{10}$ of 300   (d) three quarters of 160

   (e) $\frac{5}{8}$ of 800   (f) $\frac{2}{6}$ of 240   (g) $\frac{5}{9}$ of 450   (h) three sevenths of 280

5 Write

   (a) £$\frac{2}{10}$ in pence   (b) $\frac{9}{10}$ km in metres   (c) $\frac{3}{10}$ kg in grams

   (d) $\frac{17}{100}$ m in centimetres   (e) $\frac{9}{100}$ km in metres   (f) $\frac{5}{100}$ ℓ in millilitres.

6 (a) $\frac{4}{7}$ of 7m   (b) $\frac{9}{10}$ of 70 km   (c) $\frac{6}{8}$ of 32 ℓ (d) $\frac{3}{9}$ of 63 kg

   (e) $\frac{1}{8}$ of £4   (f) $\frac{4}{5}$ of 2 m   (g) $\frac{8}{10}$ of 7 ℓ (h) $\frac{7}{8}$ of 2 kg

7 Write the value of each stamp as a fraction of £1.

8 What fraction is (a) 70 cm of 1 m (b) 45 cm of 1 m (c) 140 cm of 1 m
   (d) 200 m of 1 km (e) 800 g of 1 kg (f) 600 ml of 1 ℓ (g) 40 ml of 1 ℓ?

627mm

371mm

789 mm

223 mm

I metre

1 How far, in thousandths of I metre, has each snail crawled?

2 Change each length to mm **or** m and mm.

(a) $\dfrac{645}{1000}$ m   (b) $\dfrac{452}{1000}$ m   (c) $2\dfrac{934}{1000}$ m   (d) $3\dfrac{578}{1000}$ m   (e) $5\dfrac{69}{1000}$ m

3 Write in thousandths of I kilometre.   (a) 817 m   (b) 304 m   (c) 87 m

4 Change each distance to m **or** km and m.

(a) $\dfrac{739}{1000}$ km   (b) $\dfrac{48}{1000}$ km   (c) $4\dfrac{488}{1000}$ km   (d) $1\dfrac{196}{1000}$ km   (e) $6\dfrac{9}{1000}$ km

5

| Hamster | Gerbil | Rat | Mouse |

Write the weight of each animal as a fraction of I kilogram.

6 Change each weight to g **or** kg and g.

(a) $\dfrac{764}{1000}$ kg   (b) $\dfrac{22}{1000}$ kg   (c) $3\dfrac{999}{1000}$ kg   (d) $7\dfrac{866}{1000}$ kg   (e) $2\dfrac{7}{1000}$ kg

1 Write True (T) of False (F) for each statement about Bill's path.

   (a) There is 1 red slab for every 3 grey slabs.

   (b) The number of red slabs is $\frac{1}{3}$ of the number of grey slabs.

   (c) The number of grey slabs is 4 times the number of red slabs.

   (d) 1 in every 4 slabs is red.
      The proportion of red slabs is $\frac{1}{4}$ of all the slabs.

   (e) 3 in every 4 slabs are grey.
      The proportion of grey slabs is $\frac{2}{3}$ of all the slabs.

2 Write **true** statements about each of these paths.

   (a) 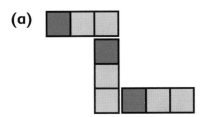   **(b)**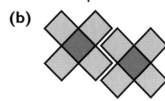

3 Bill uses slabs to make a garden design like this ⟶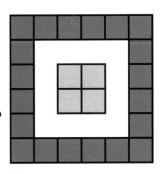

   (a) How many red slabs to grey slabs are there?
   (b) What fraction is the number of grey slabs
       of the number of red slabs?
   (c) What proportion of **all** the slabs is •grey •red?

4 For the base of a patio Bill uses
2 bags of sand to every 5 bags of grit.
He uses 21 bags altogether.
How many bags does Bill use of
(a) sand   **(b)** grit?

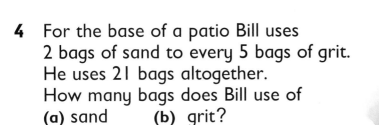

5 Concrete for the patio is mixed using 2 buckets
of cement to every 3 buckets of sand.
Bill needs 30 buckets altogether.
How many buckets of each does he need?

1 List the first eight numbers in each sequence.

(a) Start at 0. Count on 0·1 each time.

(b)  Start at 2. Count on 0·5 each time.

(c) Start at 4. Count 0·25 each time.

(d)  Start at 10. Count **back** 0·1 each time.

(e) Start at 8. Count back 0·5 each time.

(f)  Start at 6. Count back 0·25 each time.

2 Copy and complete each sequence.

(a) 0·92, 0·94, 0·96, ■, ■, ■, 1·04

(b) 1·76, 1·77, 1·78, ■, ■, ■, 1·82

(c) 2·54, 2·52, 2·50, ■, ■, ■, 2·42

(d) 3·04, 3·03, 3·02, ■, ■, ■, 2·98

3 Write the 2-place decimal fraction

(a) before 6·48   **(b)** after 7·35   **(c)** before 5·86

(d) after 3·24   **(e)** before 8·21   **(f)** after 1·69.

4 Write the 2-place decimal fraction between

(a) 0·47 and 0·49   **(b)** 3·58 and 3·60   **(c)** 5·99 and 6·01.

5 Write **a** 2-place decimal fraction between

(a) 0·67 and 0·74   **(b)** 1·81 and 1·9   **(c)** 3·9 and 4·05.

6 Write each decimal as a mixed number.

(a) 2 4 · 7   **(b)** 2 · 4 1

(c) 5 · 8 9   **(d)** 7 8 · 3

(e) 5 0 · 2   **(f)** 3 · 6 3

(g) 4 7 · 5   **(h)** 6 · 0 5

$16·3 = 16\frac{3}{10}$

$4·58 =$

30·6   45·8   3·24   6·38   1·75

4·52   13·9

I Which number has

   (a) 2 tenths   **(b)** 5 hundredths
   (c) 7 units   **(d)** 4 tens
   (e) the largest tenths digit
   (f) the smallest tenths digit
   (g) a units digit double the tenths digit
   (h) a hundredths digit half of the tenths digit?

0·46   8·07

97·4   2·63

2 Write the value of each red digit.

(a) 7 | 1 | 6   **(b)** 1 | 6 | 7   **(c)** 1 | 6 | 7

(d) 4 | 3 | 8   **(e)** 6 | 9 | 2   **(f)** 5 | 0 | 5

3 Which is the largest number?

(a) | 2·48 | 2·84 | 2·80 | **(b)** | 6·76 | 6·7 | 6·75 | **(c)** | 2·31 | 3·12 | 3·21 |

4 Which is the smallest number?

(a) | 6·51 | 6·15 | 6·5 | **(b)** | 8·75 | 8·7 | 8·57 | **(c)** | 4·3 | 4·35 | 4·53 |

5 Write the numbers in order.

  ● Start with the smallest.

(a) 0·58, 0·40, 0·53, 0·61, 0·42   **(b)** 0·2, 0·06, 0·14, 0·09, 0·1
(c) 5·99, 6·43, 4·63, 4·36, 6·34, 6·06   **(d)** 9·9, 9·01, 0·19, 9·1, 0·91, 9·09

  ● Start with the largest.

(e) 0·73, 0·62, 0·8, 0·7, 0·75   **(f)** 0·9, 1·05, 0·98, 1·08, 1·0
(g) 7·59, 9·75, 7·79, 9·95, 9·57, 7·95   **(h)** 8·8, 8·02, 0·28, 8·2, 0·82, 8·08

49

1 Write the length of each jump **to the nearest tenth of 1 metre.**

(a)  5·63 m

(b)  4·28 m

(c)  5·44 m

(d)  4·97 m

2 Write the height cleared by each pole-vaulter **to the nearest tenth of 1 metre.**

Gio	Franco	Bert	Danny
3·67 m	4·15 m	3·51 m	4·03 m

3 The table shows the results in the javelin competition.
Round each distance thrown **to the nearest whole metre.**

	Throw 1	Throw 2	Throw 3
Ellie	61·26 m	56·84 m	67·07 m
Cara	72·59 m	75·13 m	70·5 m
Alana	63·81 m	74·56 m	68·02 m

4 For each competitor, find

(a) the **approximate** total distance of Throws 1 and 2

(b) the approximate difference between Throws 1 and 2.

	Throw 1	Throw 2
Harry	16·41 m	18·3 m
Imo	12·26 m	19·85 m

 5 Repeat question **4,** this time finding the **exact** totals and differences.

50

1 (a) Find the total distance, in metres, each player's counter has jumped.
  (b) The cup is 2 metres from each player. How far, in metres, does each player's counter still have to jump to reach it?

2 Find the missing numbers.

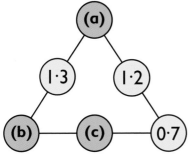

Each side of the triangle has a total of 3.

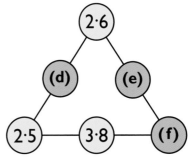

Each side of the triangle has a total of 8.

3 Find the sum of the numbers on each counter.

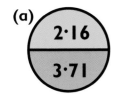
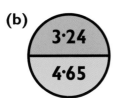
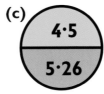
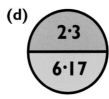
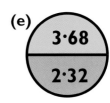

(a) 2·16 / 3·71 (b) 3·24 / 4·65 (c) 4·5 / 5·26 (d) 2·3 / 6·17 (e) 3·68 / 2·32

4 (a) 5·62 + ■ = 6   (b) ■ + 7·18 = 8   (c) 6·52 + ■ = 6·6
  (d) 2·14 + ■ = 2·2 (e) ■ + 1·32 = 4·75 (f) 2·47 + ■ = 4·87

5 Write **three** different addition stories using these numbers.
  (a) Use 2 numbers each time.
  (b) Use 4 numbers each time.

  1·06   2·7   0·4   6·48   32·3

HOME ACTIVITY 17   Decimals: mental addition

Sponsored games - money raised

Class 6

	Snakes & Ladders	Ludo	Connect 4	Beetle Drive	Tiddly-winks
Red team	£6·32	£5·51	£3·47	£21·50	£12·46
Blue team	£3·85	£7·07	£6·13	£23·35	£11·62
Yellow team	£3·62	£8·85	£5·31	£13·72	£12·02
Green team	£4·40	£4·32	£3·52	£14·33	£13·67

1 How much money did each team raise playing

(a) *Snakes and Ladders* and *Connect 4*
(b) *Ludo* and *Tiddlywinks*
(c) *Beetle Drive* and *Tiddlywinks*?

2 How much money altogether was raised
  • by the red and blue teams playing
    (a) *Snakes and Ladders*   (b) *Tiddlywinks*

  • by the yellow and green teams playing
    (c) *Snakes and Ladders*   (d) *Beetle Drive*   (e) *Ludo*?

3 Which team did each of these children play for?

(a) My team raised £40·24 altogether.

(b) My team raised the most money.

(c) My team raised between £49 and £50.

(d) My team raised £3·52 more than £40.

CHECK-UP 14

Work with a partner.

Game 1

0·75	0·42	0·3	0·89
0·9	Find the difference between a **blue** number and a **green** number.		0·13
0·56			0·98
0·21	0·67	0·34	0·8

Game 2

6·97	2·51	1·42	4·85
9·59	Subtract a **red** number from a **orange** number.		3·35
4·04			7·68
2·24	8·76	3·13	6·7

Game 3

0·65	2·76	0·25	0·92
1·45	Find pairs of numbers with a difference of 0·4.		3·56
3·16			1·05
1·32	4·36	3·96	0·52

Decimals: mental subtraction

Health Club Prices

	Swimming Pool	Multi-gym	Running Track	Raquet Sports	Ball Games
Day ticket	£6·84	£7·38	£4·52	£3·26	£2·85
Weekly ticket	£28·32	£33·89	£20·95	£11·40	£12·76
Monthly ticket	£83·28	£95·56	£73·80	£42·34	£48·04

1 Find the difference in price between
- day tickets for

    (a) the Swimming Pool and the Running Track
    (b) the Multi-gym and Raquet Sports

- weekly tickets for

    (c) Ball Games and the Multi-gym
    (d) the Running Track and Raquet Sports

- monthly tickets for

    (e) the Swimming Pool and the Multi-gym
    (f) the Running Track and Ball Games.

2 For each activity find the difference between the prices of

(a) a weekly ticket and a day ticket
(b) a monthly ticket and a weekly ticket.

3 How much does each person have left?

(a)  I had £50. I bought a weekly ticket for the Multi-gym.

(b)  I had £100. I bought a monthly ticket for Raquet Sports.

foodpack 1·2 kg

ice-axe 2·3 kg

fuel can 6·8 kg

rope 5·4 kg

water bottle 3·7 kg

1 Find the weight of

(a) 4 food packs   (b) 3 ice-axes   (c) 2 ropes

(d) 5 fuel cans   (e) 6 food packs   (f) 7 water bottles

(g) 8 ice-axes   (h) 9 ropes   (i) 3 fuel cans.

2 (a) $2 \times 3 \cdot 7 = \blacksquare$ (b) $4 \times 3 \cdot 4 = \blacksquare$ (c) $7 \times 2 \cdot 5 = \blacksquare$ (d) $8 \times 1 \cdot 9 = \blacksquare$

(e) $4 \cdot 3 \times 5 = \blacksquare$ (f) $2 \cdot 8 \times 9 = \blacksquare$ (g) $9 \cdot 1 \times 3 = \blacksquare$ (h) $3 \cdot 4 \times 6 = \blacksquare$

(i) $3 \times \blacksquare = 4 \cdot 8$ (j) $6 \times \blacksquare = 8 \cdot 4$ (k) $1 \cdot 1 \times \blacksquare = 7 \cdot 7$ (l) $2 \cdot 4 \times \blacksquare = 9 \cdot 6$

3 (a) Double 2·3   (b) Twice 1·9   (c) Double 4·6   (d) Twice 8·4

(e) $\blacksquare \times 2 = 3 \cdot 6$ (f) $\blacksquare \times 2 = 5 \cdot 2$ (g) $2 \times \blacksquare = 10 \cdot 8$ (h) $2 \times \blacksquare = 15$

4 On **Wednesday**

- Team A walked twice as far as they did on Monday
- Team B doubled the distance they walked on Tuesday.

How far did each team walk during the three days?

	Distance walked on	
	Monday	Tuesday
Team A	4·6 km	7·1 km
Team B	8·5 km	3·4 km

tent
21·3 kg

rucksack
14·2 kg

boots
1·16 kg

stove
2·51 kg

jacket
5·42 kg

1 What is the weight of

(a) 3 tents   (b) 2 rucksacks   (c) 6 pairs of boots

(d) 9 stoves   (e) 5 tents   (f) 8 jackets

(g) 3 rucksacks   (h) 6 stoves   (i) 8 tents?

2 (a) $2 \times 43{\cdot}5$ (b) $4 \times 14{\cdot}2$ (c) $7 \times 20{\cdot}1$ (d) $9 \times 10{\cdot}6$

    (e) $6{\cdot}17 \times 5$ (f) $1{\cdot}83 \times 9$ (g) $3{\cdot}64 \times 6$ (h) $4{\cdot}08 \times 7$

3 What volume of water is each climber carrying?

Anna

I have six large bottles of water.

1·43 ℓ   3·82 ℓ

I have seven small bottles of water.

I have three large bottles and two small bottles of water.

Alan

Stuart

4 The camp generator uses 37·9 litres of fuel each day.
What volume of fuel does it use in
(a) 3 days   (b) 5 days   (c) 4 days?

5 There were 300 litres of fuel in the generator's fuel tank at the start of the week.
How much fuel is left after a week's use?

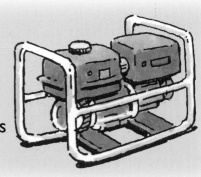

Garden Warehouse

 Bug Scram 1·6 ℓ

 Weed Zap 0·9 ℓ

 Bloom Blast 1·25 ℓ

 Leaf Shine 0·83 ℓ

1 What is the total volume of liquid in:

(a) 10    (b) 10   (c) 10    (d) 10

(e) 100    (f) 100   (g) 100   (h) 100   ?

2 (a) $10 \times 3·7$ (b) $10 \times 6·2$ (c) $18·4 \times 10$ (d) $6·41 \times 10$
  (e) $100 \times 5·9$ (f) $100 \times 78·1$ (g) $0·42 \times 100$ (h) $4·06 \times 100$
  (i) $\blacksquare \times 2·8 = 28$ (j) $0·16 \times \blacksquare = 16$ (k) $\blacksquare \times 10 = 53$ (l) $100 \times \blacksquare = 108$

3

 Pansies 6·4 g    Lobelia 3·7 g    Sweet Peas 8·1 g    Marigolds 5·9 g    Cornflowers 7·2 g

Find the weight of seeds in

(a) 20 packets of   • Pansies   • Lobelia   • Marigolds
(b) 30 packets of   • Sweet Peas   • Marigolds   • Cornflowers
(c) 70 packets of   • Pansies   • Sweet Peas   • Marigolds
(d) 90 packets of   • Lobelia   • Sweet Peas   • Cornflowers.

4 (a) $3·2 \times 40$ (b) $1·7 \times 50$ (c) $80 \times 6·3$ (d) $60 \times 7·4$
  (e) $0·51 \times 70$ (f) $0·68 \times 20$ (g) $30 \times 0·49$ (h) $50 \times 0·35$
  (i) $0·06 \times 90$ (j) $80 \times 8·6$ (k) $40 \times 10·3$ (l) $70 \times 10·2$

5 Find the total cost of 30 tomato plants and 20 strawberry plants.

 £1·40 Tomato    £0·65 Strawberry

1 Alex shares the food equally among 10 boxes.
Find the weight of food in each box.

(a) 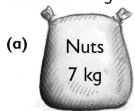 Nuts
7 kg

(b) Pasta
9 kg

(c)  Beans
15 kg

2 (a) $24 \div 10 = \blacksquare$ (b) $8 \div 10 = \blacksquare$ (c) $63 \div 10 = \blacksquare$ (d) $31 \div 10 = \blacksquare$
(e) $\blacksquare \div 10 = 0{\cdot}2$ (f) $\blacksquare \div 10 = 4{\cdot}5$ (g) $\blacksquare \div 10 = 6{\cdot}9$ (h) $\blacksquare \div 10 = 7{\cdot}1$

3 Alex shares these drinks equally among 100 bottles.
Find the volume in each bottle.

(a)  Juice
92 ℓ

(b) Milk
55 ℓ

(c)  Water
9 ℓ

4 (a) $17 \div 100 = \blacksquare$ (b) $52 \div 100 = \blacksquare$ (c) $3 \div 100 = \blacksquare$ (d) $66 \div 100 = \blacksquare$
(e) $\blacksquare \div 100 = 0{\cdot}56$ (f) $\blacksquare \div 100 = 0{\cdot}4$ (g) $\blacksquare \div 100 = 0{\cdot}73$ (h) $\blacksquare \div 100 = 0{\cdot}05$

5 (a) $15 \div \blacksquare = 1{\cdot}5$ (b) $27 \div \blacksquare = 0{\cdot}27$ (c) $6 \div \blacksquare = 0{\cdot}06$
(d) $9 \div \blacksquare = 0{\cdot}9$ (e) $51 \div \blacksquare = 5{\cdot}1$ (f) $24 \div \blacksquare = 0{\cdot}24$

6 (a) $\frac{1}{2}$ of $0{\cdot}48$ (b) half of $0{\cdot}54$ (c) $\frac{1}{2}$ of $0{\cdot}7$
(d) $\blacksquare \div 2 = 1{\cdot}5$ (e) $\blacksquare \div 2 = 3{\cdot}9$ (f) $\blacksquare \div 2 = 4{\cdot}6$

7 (a) Share 2·8 kg of dried fruit equally among 7 customers.

(b) Share 7·2 ℓ of olive oil equally among 9 customers.

8 (a) $1{\cdot}8 \div 3 = \blacksquare$ (b) $4{\cdot}2 \div 6 = \blacksquare$ (c) $6{\cdot}4 \div 8 = \blacksquare$ (d) $3{\cdot}6 \div 4 = \blacksquare$
(e) $3{\cdot}5 \div \blacksquare = 0{\cdot}7$ (f) $5{\cdot}4 \div \blacksquare = 0{\cdot}6$ (g) $2{\cdot}8 \div \blacksquare = 0{\cdot}7$ (h) $5{\cdot}6 \div \blacksquare = 0{\cdot}8$

1 Share these amounts of compost equally.

(a) 22·4 kg among 7 pots
(b) 31·2 kg among 4 pots
(c) 59·2 kg among 8 pots
(d) 48 kg among 5 pots.

2 Find the amount of fertilizer for one tree.

(a) 25·8 litres for 6 oak trees
(b) 33·3 litres for 9 pine trees
(c) 53·7 litres for 3 elm trees
(d) 86·1 litres for 7 ash trees.

3 Find the cost of one of each item.

(a)

5 flowerpots
cost £8·65

(b)

2 sets of windchimes
cost £9·38

(c)

8 tulip bulbs
cost £1·52

(d)

3 gnomes
cost £7·41

(e)

9 candles
cost £5·22

(f)

6 plants
cost £4·32

4 Which is cheaper, a chair
or a stool?
Explain.

4 chairs £9·40

3 stools £7·65

I Anna's baggage weighs **8·247 kg** or **$8\frac{247}{1000}$ kg** or **8247 thousandths of 1 k**

Write each of these weights in other ways.

(a)
```
Kilograms
1.576
```

(b)
```
Kilograms
0.449
```

(c)
```
Kilograms
9.704
```

(d)
```
Kilograms
0.608
```

(e)
```
Kilograms
0.123
```

(f)
```
Kilograms
5.851
```

(g)
```
Kilograms
0.037
```

(h)
```
Kilograms
6.005
```

2 Write each weight in decimal form.

(a) $\frac{982}{1000}$ kg   (b) $\frac{566}{1000}$ kg   (c) $\frac{17}{1000}$ kg   (d) 309 thousandths of 1 kg

(e) $2\frac{294}{1000}$ kg   (f) $7\frac{473}{1000}$ kg   (g) $4\frac{5}{1000}$ kg   (h) 8708 thousandths of 1 kg

3 Copy and complete each sequence.

(a) 0·347, 0·348, 0·349, ___, ___, ___, 0·353
(b) 1·094, 1·096, 1·098, ___, ___, ___, 1·106
(c) 0·716, 0·712, 0·708, ___, ___, ___, 0·692
(d) 3·515, 3·510, 3·505, ___, ___, ___, 3·485
(e) 0·283, 0·483, 0·683, ___, ___, ___, 1·483
(f) 4·199, 4·298, 4·397, ___, ___, ___, 4·793

4 Write the 3-place decimal fraction between

(a) 0·124 and 0·126   (b) 3·817 and 3·819
(c) 6·305 and 6·307   (d) 5·032 and 5·034

5 Write a 3-place decimal fraction between

(a) 0·997 and 1·002   (b) 1·231 and 1·321
(c) 9·589 and 9·6   (d) 4·45 and 4·46

1 What is the value of the green digit in each display?

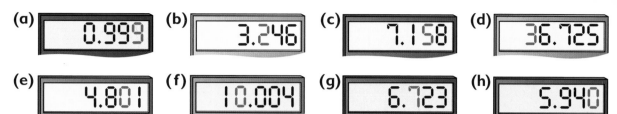

(a) 0.999 (b) 3.246 (c) 7.158 (d) 36.725

(e) 4.801 (f) 10.004 (g) 6.723 (h) 5.940

2 Which number on the cards has

(a) 8 thousandths (b) 6 tenths
(c) 7 hundredths (d) 4 tens
(e) the largest thousandths digit
(f) the smallest thousandths digit
(g) a thousandths digit half of the tenths digit?

40·294	9·246	0·687
8·073	0·864	4·902
6·489	0·768	8·726

3 Write each number as a 3-place decimal fraction.

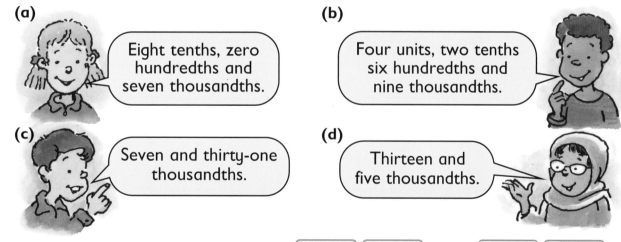

(a) Eight tenths, zero hundredths and seven thousandths.

(b) Four units, two tenths six hundredths and nine thousandths.

(c) Seven and thirty-one thousandths.

(d) Thirteen and five thousandths.

4 Which is the larger number? (a) 7·373 7·337 (b) 4·008 4·080

5 Which is the smaller number? (a) 3·069 3·69 (b) $5\frac{30}{1000}$ 5·3

6 Write the numbers in order.

- Start with the smallest.
  (a) 4·543, 5·543, 5·534, 5·453, 4·554 (b) 9·987, 8·998, 9·978, 8·987, 9·897
- Start with the largest.
  (c) 2·201, 2·102, 1·21, 2·212, 1·212 (d) 6·5, 7·556, 6·765, 7·5, 7·65

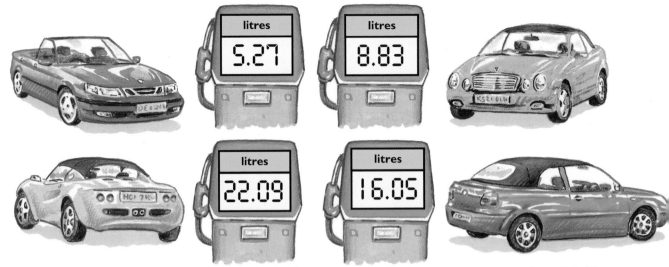

1 Write the reading on each fuel pump **to the nearest tenth of 1 litre.**

2 Write each of these volumes to the nearest tenth of 1 litre.

(a)
litres
0.416

(b)
litres
3.782

(c)
litres
14.055

(d)
litres
37.006

3

	Lap 1	Lap 2
	41·2 s	37·5 s
	48·91 s	43·67 s
	39·497 s	39·501 s
	52·086 s	54·742 s

The table shows the **practice** lap times, in seconds, for each car.

List the lap times for each rounded to the nearest **whole number** of seconds.

4 These are the cars' **race** times in seconds.

Lap 1	40·7 s	47·09 s	36·168 s	53·004 s
Lap 2	36·2 s	41·83 s	29·522 s	59·519 s

For each car, round the race times to the nearest whole number of seconds then find
(a) it's **approximate** total time for Lap 1 and Lap 2
(b) the **approximate** difference between its times for Lap 1 and Lap 2.

5 Find the **exact** totals and differences in questions **4 (a)** and **4 (b)**.

Decimals: rounding and approximating

← 12·096 m →

← 4·125 m →

← 9·703 m →

1 Write the length of each vehicle in **millimetres.**

2 Change

(a) 1·842 km to m   (b) 0·638 ℓ to ml   (c) 7·001 kg to g
(d) 5·287 tonnes to kg   (e) 3474 m to km   (f) 369 mm to m
(g) 2050 ml to ℓ   (h) 6509 g to kg.

3 Give each answer in decimal form.

(a) Find the total top-up volume of
 • engine oil   • screen wash

(b) Find the difference between
the top-up volumes of
 • engine oil   • screen wash.

Top - up volumes		
	engine oil	screen wash
	2·3 ℓ	425 ml
	500 ml	3·55 ℓ

4 Write each fraction in decimal form then check by dividing.

(a) $\frac{1}{10}$ (b) $\frac{9}{10}$ (c) $\frac{1}{2}$ (d) $\frac{1}{5}$ (e) $\frac{1}{4}$ (f) $\frac{3}{4}$

(g) $\frac{1}{100}$ (h) $\frac{3}{100}$ (i) $\frac{75}{100}$ (j) $\frac{1}{1000}$ (k) $\frac{467}{1000}$ (l) $\frac{74}{1000}$

5 Find, by dividing, the decimal form of each of these fractions.

(a) $\frac{1}{8}$ (b) $\frac{11}{40}$ (c) $\frac{3}{16}$ (d) $\frac{1}{3}$ (e) $\frac{1}{9}$ (f) $\frac{4}{9}$

6 Find the larger fraction by changing both to decimal form.

(a) $\frac{3}{8}$ $\frac{2}{5}$ (b) $\frac{9}{10}$ $\frac{8}{9}$ (c) $\frac{2}{7}$ $\frac{1}{3}$

7 List these fractions in order, starting with the smallest.

$\frac{27}{40}$ $\frac{5}{8}$ $\frac{2}{3}$ $\frac{13}{20}$

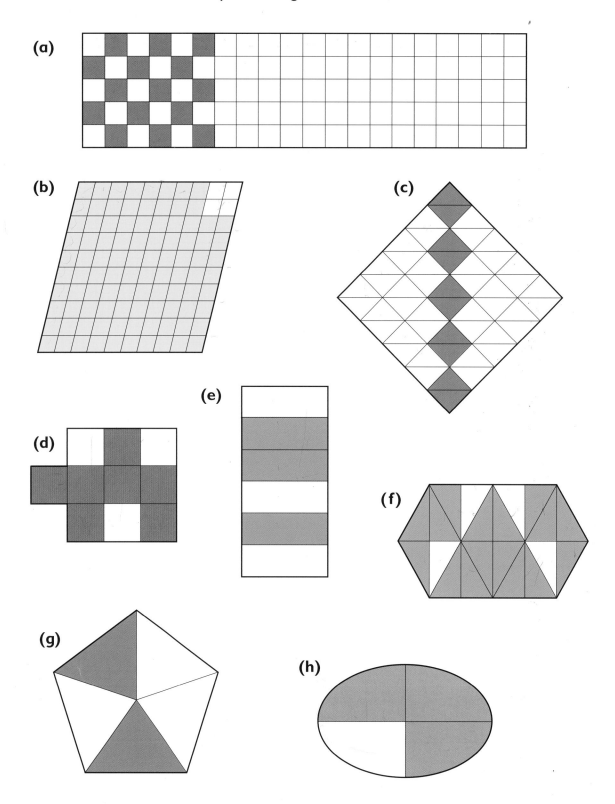

I For each shape, write the amount coloured
as a fraction **and** as a percentage.

(a)

(b)

(c)

(d)

(e)

(f)

(g)

(h)

1 Write as a fraction **and** as a percentage.

   (a) 31 out of 100   **(b)** 30 out of 60   **(c)** 20 out of 200

   (d) 100 out of 500   **(e)** 7 out of 100   **(f)** 50 out of 1000

2 Find the **percentage**

   (a) **not** cotton   **(b)** **not** wool   **(c)** **not** nylon.

ninety-five
hundredths
cotton

six tenths
wool

four fifths
nylon

3 Find.

   (a) 10 % of 30   **(b)** 20 % of 100   **(c)** 50 % of 500

   (d) 40 % of 70   **(e)** 30 % of 90   **(f)** 70 % of 40

   (g) 80 % of 20   **(h)** 60 % of 200   **(i)** 100 % of 60

4 Which bottle contains the greatest volume of **fresh orange**?

5 What percentage of each *Growalot* bag is **soil**?

6 Find the weight of
   • fertiliser   • compost   • sand
in **400 kg** of *Growalot*.

GROWALOT

10 % fertiliser

40 % compost

25 % sand

% soil

1 Write as a percentage.

   (a)   9 out of 90   (b)   7 out of 35   (c)   60 out of 80

   (d) 15 out of 60   (e) 14 out of 70   (f)   23 out of 46

   (g)   4 out of 10   (h)   1 out of 20   (i)   17 out of 50

2 **(a)** How many test questions did Kelly answer incorrectly?

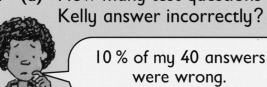

10 % of my 40 answers were wrong.

Kelly

(b) For what length of the race was Liam in the lead?

I led for 25 % of the 1 kilometre race.

Liam

(c) How much money did Sunil spend?

I spent 25 % of my £300 savings.

Sunil

(d) How much money did Gaby give to her sister?

I gave 30 % of my £5 pocket money to my sister.

Gaby

(e) What length of Una's rope is frayed?

40 % of this 3 metre rope is frayed.

Una

(f) How many of Adam's stamps are British?

75 % of my 200 stamps are British.

Adam

(g) What weight of potatoes has Harry?

I have 5 kilograms of vegetables. 70 % are potatoes.

Harry

(h) What volume of Lucy's punch is orange juice?

I made 30 litres of fruit punch. $33\frac{1}{3}$ % is orange juice.

Lucy

3 Find

   (a)   5 % of 80   (b) 15 % of 60   (c)   13 % of 200

   (d) $12\frac{1}{2}$ % of 1600   (e) $2\frac{1}{2}$ % of 120   (f) 11 % of 1000.

1 Write as a percentage.

(a) 0·15   (b) $\frac{3}{10}$ (c) 0·91   (d) $\frac{7}{20}$ (e) 0·06   (f) $\frac{9}{50}$

2 Write in two other ways.

(a) 43 %   (b) $\frac{8}{25}$ (c) 0·7   (d) $\frac{3}{5}$ (e) 8 %   (f) 0·12

3 (a) Which of these numbers is equivalent to 65 %?

6·5	$6\frac{1}{5}$	0·65	65·0

(b) Which of these percentages is the equivalent to 0·27?

0·27 %	2·7 %	27 %	270 %

4 Which is greater

(a) 37 % or $\frac{4}{10}$ (b) 0·8 or 75 %   (c) 22 % or 2·2   (d) $\frac{1}{20}$ or 20 %?

5 Write True (T) or False (F).

(a) 30 % < $\frac{2}{5}$ (b) 0·1 > 11 %   (c) $\frac{40}{50}$ < 70 %   (d) 10 % > 0·01

6 Write the numbers which are

(a) greater than one half	$\frac{3}{4}$	38 %	$\frac{3}{8}$	0·6	55 %
(b) smaller than one quarter.	0·3	24 %	$\frac{4}{20}$	0·26	40 %

7 List in order, starting with the **smallest** number.

| 9 | 99 | 9 % | 0·9 | 99 % |

8 Copy and complete each sequence.

(a) 10 %, 0·15, $\frac{20}{100}$, 25 %, ___ , ___ , ___ , 0·45, $\frac{50}{100}$

(b) $\frac{20}{100}$, 0·18, 16 %, ___ , 0·12, ___ , ___ , ___ , 4 %

1 A school group of fifty people is visiting the London Eye.
- 10 % are adults
- 58 % are girls

How many are **boys**?

2 Bigcity United's ticket prices are about to rise by 5 %.
What will the new price of this ticket be?

3 Sixty fair-haired children are 30 % of the total number who attend Brockley School.
How many children altogether attend the school?

4 Bigcity United played thirty games last season.
They won 60 % of these.
How many games did they **lose**?

DAILY BLAH Monday 3 January

UNITED WIN AGAIN!

5

Jamie

I had twenty-four out of thirty-two questions correct in a sports quiz.

I was correct in one hundred and forty-eight questions out of two hundred in a pop music quiz.

Roz

Who had the greater **percentage** of questions correct?

6

£40

£50

£20

£30

| **Discount Vouchers** |
| **Half price** any item costing less than £50 |
| **Take 10% off** any item |
| **Take £6 off** any item |

What is the **cheapest** total cost of the four items, using the *Discount Vouchers*? Explain.

1   Write the weight of each item in kilograms, to the nearest $\frac{1}{10}$ kg **and** in grams, to the nearest 100 g.

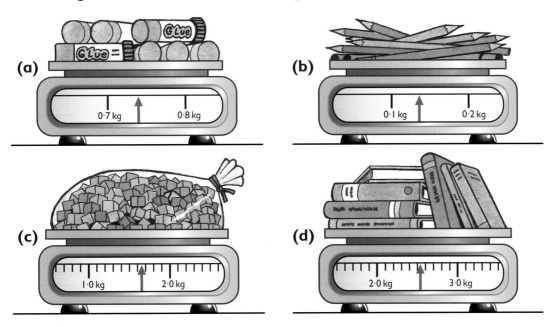

(a)   0·7 kg   0·8 kg

(b)   0·1 kg   0·2 kg

(c)   1·0 kg   2·0 kg

(d)   2·0 kg   3·0 kg

2   Write each weight in grams, to the nearest 100 g **and** in kilograms, to the nearest $\frac{1}{10}$ kg.

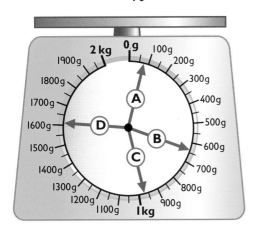

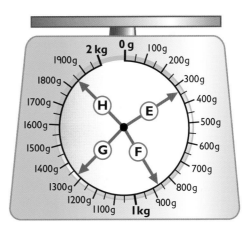

3   Find the weight of some containers
    • in grams, to the nearest 100 g
    • in kilograms, to the nearest $\frac{1}{10}$ kg.

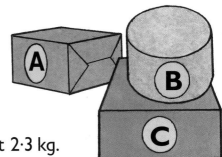

4   Find an object that weighs
    (a)   between 0·8 kg and 1·0 kg   (b)   about 2·3 kg.

1 (a) Weigh an empty school bag.
  (b) Estimate how much the bag will weigh when it contains

  - a reading book, a maths book and a pencil case

  - 3 library books, 4 exercise books and a pair of trainers.

  (c) Use a spring balance or scales to check each estimate.

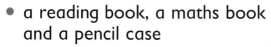

2 Put some objects into a school bag so that its total weight is between 4 kg 800 g and 5 kg 100 g.

3 Write the weight of each object in grams.

(a) 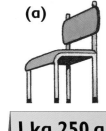 (b) (c)  (d)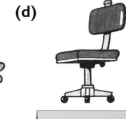

| (a) 1 kg 250 g | (b) 3 kg 125 g | (c) 4 kg 568 g | (d) 2 kg 379 g |

4 Write the weight of each object in kilograms and grams.

(a)  (b) 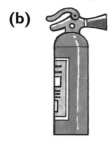 (c) 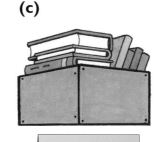 (d)

| (a) 5482 g | (b) 7634 g | (c) 9513 g | (d) 6747 g |

5 Write each weight in another way.

(a) 7 kg 132 g   (b) 8716 g   (c) 4 kg 303 g   (d) 6948 g
(e) 1 kg 255 g   (f) 5681 g   (g) 2 kg 569 g   (h) 9074 g

1 Write each weight in kilograms.

(a)

11 tonnes 950 kg

(b)

34 tonnes 750 kg

(c)

4 tonnes 500 kg

2 Write each weight in tonnes and kilograms.

(a)

5900 kg

(b)

3300 kg

(c)

13 950 kg

3 A single-decker bus weighs about 8500 kg.
Fourteen adults have a total weight
of about 1 tonne.
There are 42 adults on the bus.
What is the approximate total
weight of the bus and its
passengers in kilograms?

4

Sleepers 90 kg each

Slabs 20 kg each

Gravel 500 kg bag

An unloaded truck weighs 5 tonnes.
When it leaves the depot it is
transporting:

- 4 bags of gravel
- 100 paving slabs
- 20 railway sleepers.

What is the truck's **total** loaded
weight in tonnes and kilograms?

5 (a) Find the total weight of the children in your class.

(b) How many kilograms more or less than 1 tonne is this total weight?

1 Measure each bird in centimetres then calculate its true length.

Scale: 1 cm to 3 cm

(a) Firecrest   **(b) Robin**   **(c) Goldfinch**

(d) Little Grebe   **(e) Sandpiper**

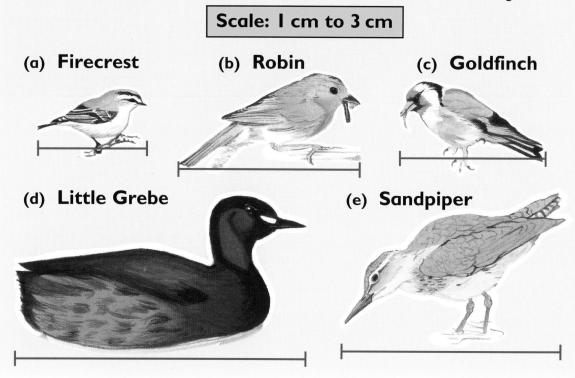

2 Each bird is drawn to a different scale.

   (a) Measure each wingspan in centimetres then calculate the length of the true wingspan.

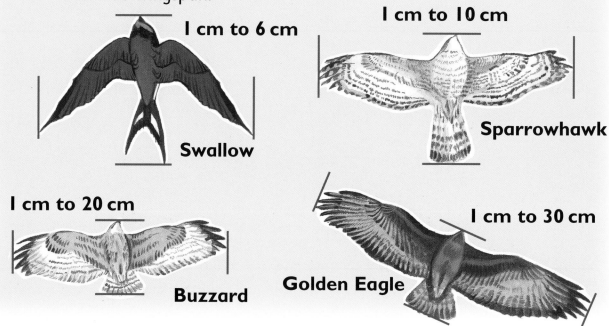

1 cm to 6 cm

1 cm to 10 cm

Swallow

Sparrowhawk

1 cm to 20 cm

1 cm to 30 cm

Buzzard

Golden Eagle

   (b) Find the true **body length** of each bird.

1 This plan of the aviary is drawn to a scale of **1 cm to 2 m**.
Find the true length and breadth of each part.

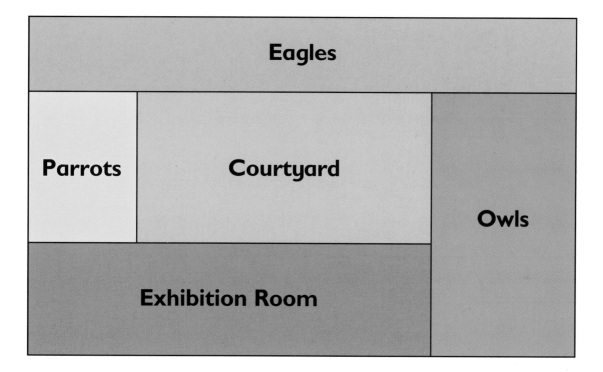

2 These trees grow near the aviary.

(a) Find the true height of each tree.

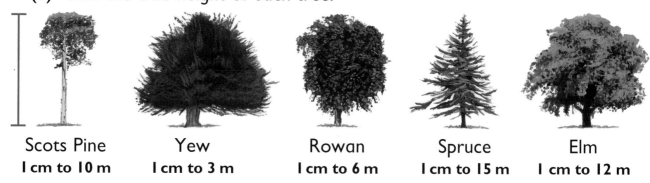

Scots Pine	Yew	Rowan	Spruce	Elm
1 cm to 10 m	1 cm to 3 m	1 cm to 6 m	1 cm to 15 m	1 cm to 12 m

(b) Sketch each tree using a scale of **1 cm to 3 m**.

1 Measure and record each caterpillar's length
- in millimetres only
- in centimetres and millimetres.

(a)    **(b)** 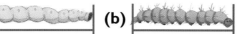   **(c)**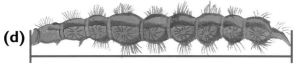

(d)    **(e)**

2 Write in millimetres.
(a) 3 cm 7 mm   **(b)** 15 cm 9 mm   **(c)** 8 cm 1 mm   **(d)** 10 cm 4 mm

3 Write in centimetres and millimetres.
(a) 58 mm   **(b)** 16 mm   **(c)** 153 mm   **(d)** 205 mm

4 The wingspan of the butterfly is
32 mm or 3 cm 2 mm or 3·2 cm.

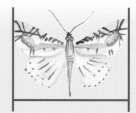

Measure each wingspan in millimetres.
Write each measurement in **three** ways.

(a)    **(b)**    **(c)**

5 Draw caterpillars with lengths of
(a) 26 mm   **(b)** 4·3 cm   **(c)** 7·4 cm   **(d)** 58 mm

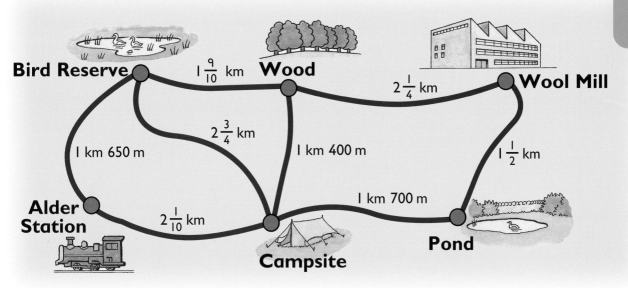

Bird Reserve — $1\frac{9}{10}$ km — **Wood** — $2\frac{1}{4}$ km — **Wool Mill**

$2\frac{3}{4}$ km

1 km 650 m

1 km 400 m

$1\frac{1}{2}$ km

1 km 700 m

Alder Station

$2\frac{1}{10}$ km — **Campsite**

Pond

1 Write **in metres** the shortest distance between

(a) the Wood and the Pond
(b) the Mill and the Campsite
(c) the Station and the Wood
(d) the Bird Reserve and the Pond.

2 Find the total distance, in metres, of each of these journeys.

(a) Station ⟶ Bird Reserve ⟶ Wood ⟶ Mill
(b) Wood ⟶ Mill ⟶ Pond ⟶ Campsite
(c) Mill ⟶ Wood ⟶ Campsite ⟶ Bird Reserve

3 The distance from Alder to Linton is 6 km 300 m.

Write the distance, in kilometres and metres, from

(a) Bagley to Entworth
(b) Bagley to Linton
(c) Alder to Bagley
(d) Linton to Entworth.

	Linton	Entworth	Bagley
Alder	6300 m	7423 m	4008 m
Bagley	9040 m	4180 m	
Entworth	5706 m		

4 (a) Which two reels of wool have a total length of $7\frac{1}{2}$ km?

(b) Which three reels have a total length of 11 km?

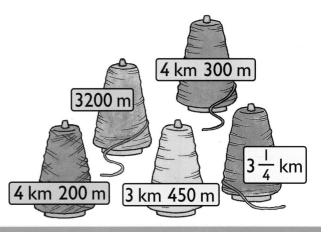

4 km 300 m

3200 m

$3\frac{1}{4}$ km

4 km 200 m

3 km 450 m

1 Which of these is likely to be the best estimate for each length?

| about 100 m | about 10 mm | about 1 m | about 1 km | about 10 m | about 100 km | about 10 cm | about 5 m |

length of
a belt

length of
a car

width of
a calculator

height of
a lamppost

length of an
airport runway

width of
a button

distance from
Newcastle to York

length of
a train

2 Which of these lengths would you measure in

(a) kilometres   **(b)** metres   **(c)** centimetres   **(d)** millimetres?

length of
a bus

height of
a tree

wingspan of
a midge

distance from the
Earth to the Moon

length of
a motorway

length of
a pencil

thickness of
a coin

height of
a house

3 Suggest two other items you would measure in

(a) kilometres   **(b)** metres   **(c)** centimetres   **(d)** millimetres.

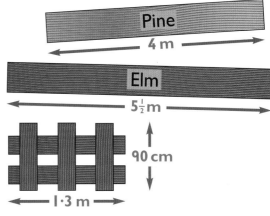

1 Find the length of wood left when

  (a) 35 cm is cut from the pine

  (b) 1 m 65 cm is cut from the elm.

2 Find the total length of wood used to make this section of fencing.

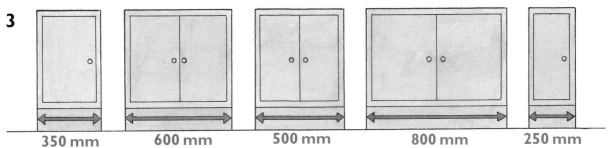

3

(a) How wide are the cupboards each person should buy?

I need two cupboards with a total width of 140 cm.

Dave

I need three cupboards with a total width of 120 cm.

Senga

  (b) Which four **different** cupboards will fit into a space two metres wide?

4 Find the total distance travelled by Jim's van during the week.

	distance travelled
Monday	3 km
Tuesday	6700 m
Wednesday	4 km 450 m
Thursday	5·5 km
Friday	2800 m

1 **Measure** to find each perimeter. Write it
- in millimetres only
- in centimetres only.

(a)

(b)
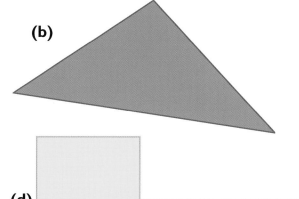

(c)
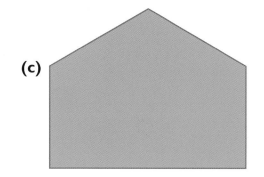

(d)
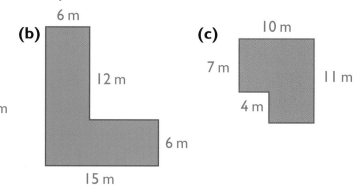

2 **Calculate** the perimeter of each shape.

(a) 10 m, 15 m, 16 m, 11 m

(b) 6 m, 12 m, 6 m, 15 m

(c) 10 m, 7 m, 11 m, 4 m

(d) 4 m, 4 m, 6 m, 4 m, 5 m

(e) 10 m, 12 m, 8 m, 14 m, 39 m

3 Find the true perimeter of this shape.

Scale: 1 cm to 2 m

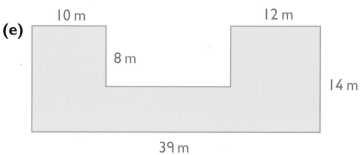

1 **Measure** in millimetres to find the perimeter of each rectangle.

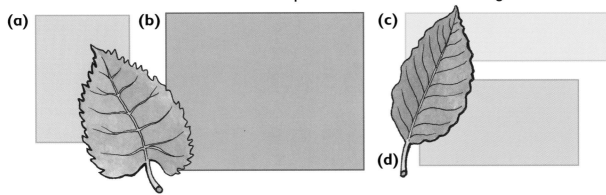

(a) **(b)** **(c)**

(d)

2 How can you calculate the perimeter of a rectangle when you know its length and breadth?

3 **Calculate** the perimeter of each rectangle.

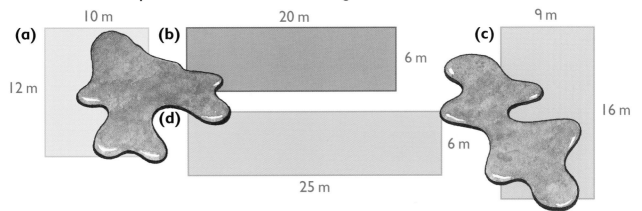

(a) 10 m **(b)** 20 m **(c)** 9 m

12 m 6 m

(d) 16 m

6 m

25 m

4 New fencing is to be put up around the perimeter of each enclosure at City Farm. Calculate the length of fencing needed for

(a) the deer park - length 30 m, breadth 25 m
(b) the cow field - length 45 m, breadth 22 m
(c) the sheep pen - length 27 m, breadth 18 m.

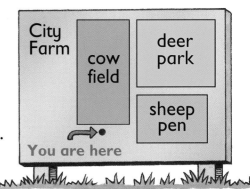

City Farm

cow field

deer park

sheep pen

You are here

5 The City Farm
- is rectangular in shape
- is 65 metres long and 60 metres wide
- has a perimeter wall.

Calculate the length of the wall.

1 Write each time as a 24-hour time.

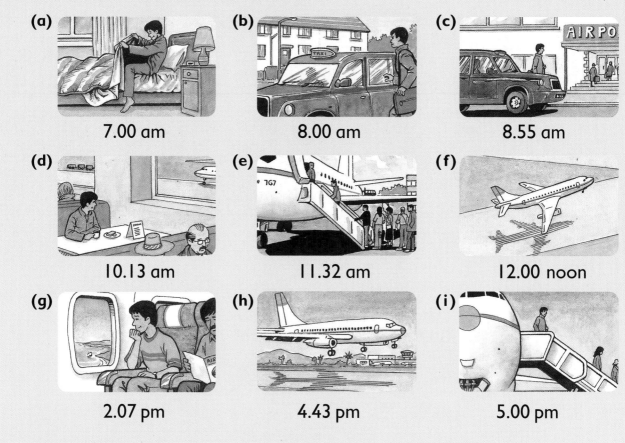

(a) 7.00 am

(b) 8.00 am

(c) 8.55 am

(d) 10.13 am

(e) 11.32 am

(f) 12.00 noon

(g) 2.07 pm

(h) 4.43 pm

(i) 5.00 pm

2 Where was Gavin at each of these times?

(a) 06.58   (b) 08.26   (c) 11.31   (d) 15.03   (e) 16.52

3 Write each time as a 12-hour time. Use am or pm.

(a) 04.00   (b) 22.00   (c) 02.15   (d) 19.45   (e) 23.09
(f) 00.23   (g) 20.36   (h) 18.51   (i) 01.11   (j) 00.00

4 What is the destination of the flight which departs

(a) at 5 am   (b) at 9.35 pm
(c) just before 1.30 pm   (d) just after 6 am
(e) just after 8.10 pm   (f) just before 5.45 pm
(g) between 8.15 am and 11.15 am
(h) between noon and 12.30 pm?

Flight Departures	
Aberdeen	1327
Belfast	0601
Bristol	2135
Dublin	1227
Edinburgh	0500
Glasgow	2011
Manchester	1744
Newcastle	0935

5 Draw the Departures board with the flights in order of take-off times.

Local Time Around the World

New York	Bermuda	London	Athens	Bombay	Beijing	Adelaide
07:00	09:00	12:00	14:00	17:30	20:00	21:30

1 How many hours ahead of or behind the time in London is each local time?

2 When it is 14.30 in London what is the local time in

    (a) Athens   **(b)** Bombay   **(c)** Bermuda?

3 For each of these local times, give the time in London.

    Beijing   **Adelaide**   **New York**

    (a) 23:00   **(b)** 17:30   **(c)** 06:00

4 The time in New York is 03.00. What is the local time in

    (a) Athens   **(b)** Bermuda   **(c)** Bombay?

5 **(a)** A flight from London to Rome takes 3 hours. The flight takes off at 07.30. Local time in Rome is 1 hour ahead of London time. What is the local time when the plane lands in Rome?

    (b) Find the local landing time for each of these flights from London.

Destination	Cyprus	Moscow	Washington	San Francisco
Flying time	$4\frac{3}{4}$ h	$3\frac{1}{2}$ h	8 h	$11\frac{1}{2}$ h
Take-off time	09.00	09.45	14.00	17.30
Difference between local and London times	+2h	+4h	−5h	−8h

1 What is the time

(a) 15 minutes after... 10:50

(b) 50 minutes later than... 12:35

(c) 75 minutes later than... 17:25

(d) 1 hour and 20 minutes after... 21:55

(e) 100 min later than 06.45

(f) 1h and 55 min after 22.40?

2 What is the time

(a) 25 minutes before... 07:15

(b) 45 minutes earlier than... 10:05

(c) 100 minutes earlier than... 19:40

(d) 1 hour and 35 minutes before... 12:00

(e) 85 min earlier than 18.50

(f) 1h and 50 min before 01.30?

3 How many minutes are there between the **Start** and **Finish** times for each event?

24 - hour Sport-a-thon	Start	Finish
(a) running	05.15	06.30
(b) jumping	08.25	09.55
(c) swimming	11.05	12.45

24 - hour Sport-a-thon	Start	Finish
(d) cycling	13.10	15.00
(e) throwing	20.20	22.05
(f) walking	23.25	02.20

1

The Bruce family set out at 07.40. They arrived in the old town of Ambertini at 09.05. How long did their journey take?

2

They spent 85 minutes exploring Ambertini. At what time did they leave?

3

The journey from Ambertini to Cala took 65 minutes. At what time did the Bruce family arrive in Cala?

4

Mr and Mrs Bruce took a boat trip which left at 11.45 and lasted for 1 hour and 20 minutes. When did they arrive back in Cala?

5

Lucy and Harry went to the Water Sports Club from 11.35 to 13.20. How long did they spend at the club?

6

The family spent 1 hour and 55 minutes eating lunch then looking around Cala. They left Cala at 15.25. When did they start lunch?

7

The Bruce family arrived in Rivera for the Fiesta at 17.00. They returned to their holiday home at 23.10 after a 35 minute drive. How long did they spend at the Fiesta?

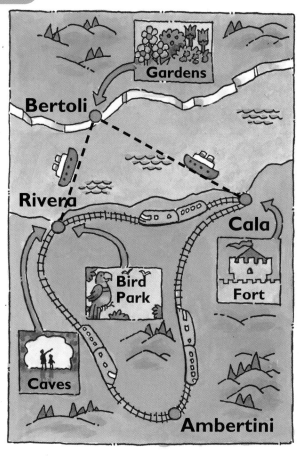

Train:	Ambertini - Cala - Rivera			
Dep	Ambertini	0710	1135	1550
Arr	Cala	0815	1250	1700
Dep	Cala	0820	1310	1715
Arr	Rivera	0915	1400	1820
Dep	Rivera	0925	1405	1825
Arr	Ambertini	1040	1535	1945

Boat:	Cala - Bertoli			
Dep	Cala	0905	1310	1740
Arr	Bertoli	0945	1400	1820
Dep	Bertoli	0955	1420	1835
Arr	Cala	1040	1505	1915

Boat:	Rivera - Bertoli			
Dep	Rivera	0920	1410	1830
Arr	Bertoli	0940	1435	1850
Dep	Bertoli	1010	1455	1905
Arr	Rivera	1035	1515	1935

1 The Bruce family travelled by train from Ambertini to Cala.
The journey took 1 hour and 15 minutes. Which train did they catch?

2 The family took a boat from Cala to Bertoli and then another boat
from Bertoli to Rivera. They arrived in Rivera at 15.15.
How long did they spend in Bertoli?

3 **(a)** How long did they have to wait for a train back to Ambertini?
    (b) At what time did they arrive in Ambertini?

4 Is it possible to take a train from Ambertini to Cala, then go by boat
to Rivera via Bertoli and travel back by train to Ambertini in time for
tea at 16.15? Explain.

5 Lucy and Harry plan a day trip from
Ambertini spending the time shown
at the Gardens and at least two
other places.

Describe their journey.

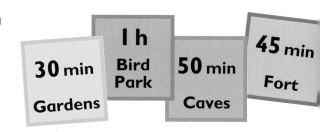

1 Copy and complete this table to show the cooking times.

Cooking time \ Weight	1 kg	$1\frac{1}{4}$ kg	$1\frac{1}{2}$ kg	$1\frac{3}{4}$ kg	2 kg	$2\frac{1}{4}$ kg	$2\frac{1}{2}$ kg
Chicken	40 min						
Lamb	48 min						
Beef	60 min						

2 Cedric, the chef, is serving lunch at 1 pm.
What is the **latest** time he can start cooking

(a) 2 kg of chicken   **(b)** $2\frac{1}{2}$ kg of beef

(c) $1\frac{3}{4}$ kg of lamb?

3 How long would you expect Cedric to take to
(a) boil an egg ⟶ 30min **or** 15 min **or** 3 min?

(b) cook vegetable casserole ⟶ 1 hour **or** 3 hours **or** 6 hours?

(c) bake a fruit cake ⟶ $1\frac{1}{2}$ hours **or** 8 hours **or** 16 hours?

4

Cedric's break times	breakfast 20 min	morning coffee 15 min	lunch 35 min	dinner 1 h	supper 20 min

Cedric works for 5 days each week.
How much break time does he have altogether in 5 days?

5 Cleo, the assistant chef, is 21 years old. Has she lived for more or less than
(a) 1000 weeks   **(b)** 8000 days   **(c)** 183 000 hours?

Explain.

1 For how many seconds has each person been exercising?

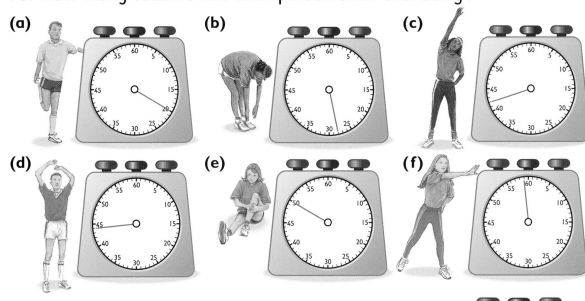

(a)

(b)

(c)

(d)

(e)

(f)

2

Elsa has been running for
18 minutes and 34 seconds.

How long has Elsa spent on each activity?

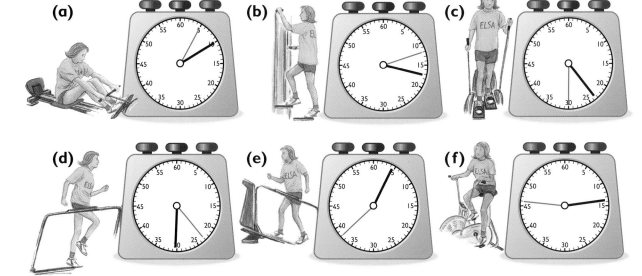

(a)

(b)

(c)

(d)

(e)

(f)

Work in pairs.

1 Use a stopclock or a watch which measures time in seconds.

(a) You have **15 seconds** for each activity.

How many times can you

- write this set of letters

  a e i o u

- toss and catch a coin

(b) You have **30 seconds** for each activity.

How many

- pegs can you put on a pegboard

- numbers can you list in order, starting at 100?

  100, 101, 102, 103, ...

(c) You have **1 minute** for each activity.

How many

- stick people can you draw

- times can you write this word?

  challenge

2 Copy the table.

(a) Estimate then measure, in seconds, the time **you** take to complete each activity.

(b) Complete the table for your results.

Activity	Time taken	
	Estimate	Measure
20 toe-touches		
50 skips		
30 bench-steps		
40 hops		

1 This is a plan of the Rexcon factory.
Calculate the area of the

    (a) Assembly Line

    (b) Paint Shed

    (c) Parts Store

    (d) Whole factory.

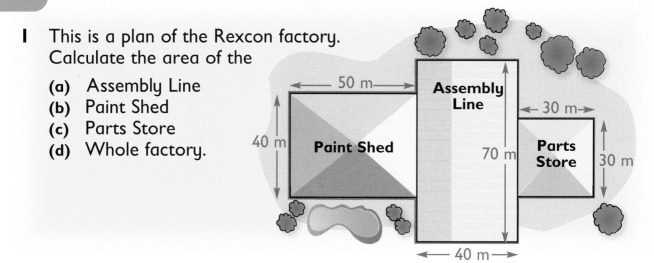

2 This is a plan of Mason's farm.
Calculate the **total** area of the farm buildings.

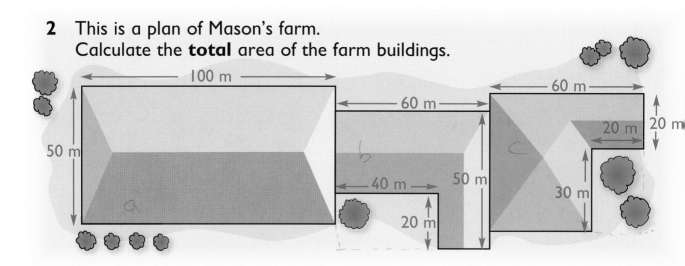

3 For each shape, **measure** side lengths then **calculate** the area.

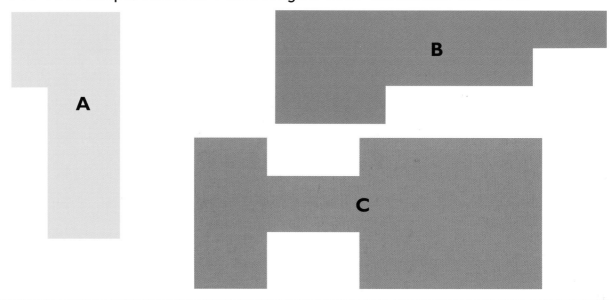

1 Calculate the area of each triangular sail.

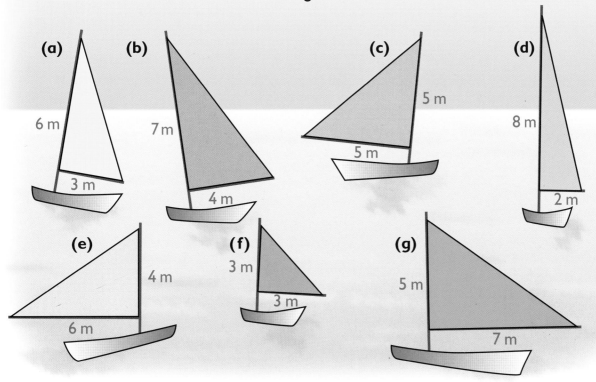

(a) 6 m, 3 m

(b) 7 m, 4 m

(c) 5 m, 5 m

(d) 8 m, 2 m

(e) 4 m, 6 m

(f) 3 m, 3 m

(g) 5 m, 7 m

2 **Measure** side lengths of these triangles then **calculate** the area of each.

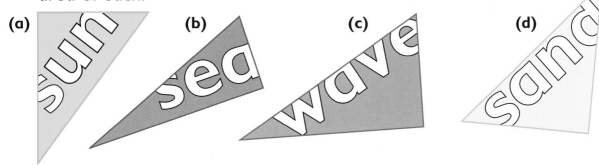

(a) sun

(b) sea

(c) wave

(d) sand

3 Calculate the **total** area of each boat design.

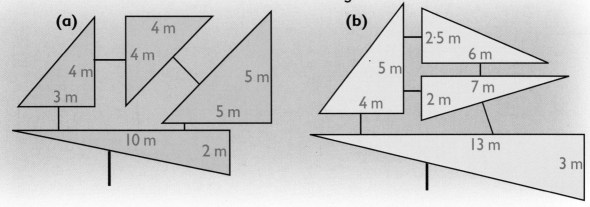

(a) 4 m, 4 m, 4 m, 3 m, 5 m, 5 m, 10 m, 2 m

(b) 2·5 m, 6 m, 5 m, 7 m, 4 m, 2 m, 13 m, 3 m

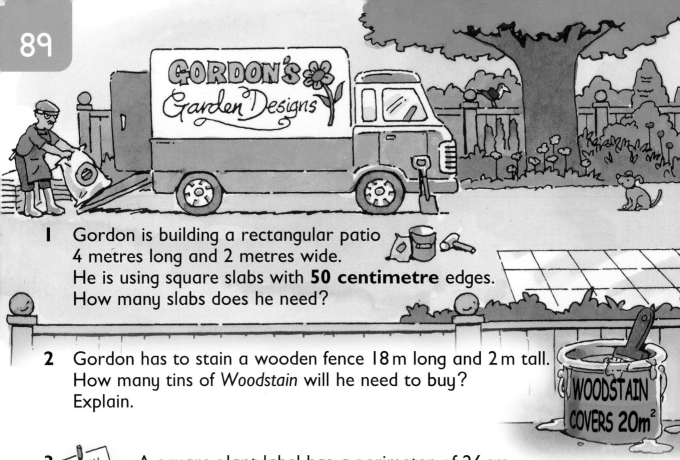

1 Gordon is building a rectangular patio
4 metres long and 2 metres wide.
He is using square slabs with **50 centimetre** edges.
How many slabs does he need?

2 Gordon has to stain a wooden fence 18 m long and 2 m tall.
How many tins of *Woodstain* will he need to buy?
Explain.

3 A square plant label has a perimeter of 24 cm.
What is its area?

4 A rectangular vegetable patch has
a perimeter of 30 m.
Its **shorter** sides are each 5 m long.
What is the area of the vegetable patch?

5 Gordon has 48 square metres of turf to make
a rectangular lawn.
List the dimensions of different rectangles he
could make.

6 Gordon's plan shows a new flower bed.
- It is an **L**-shaped hexagon.
- Four of its sides are 2 m long and
  two of its sides are 4 m long.

Sketch Gordon's flower bed on squared paper
and find its area.

TOPIC ASSESSMENT

1 Write the capacity of each container
- **in millilitres**

(a)  $\frac{7}{10} \ell$

(b) 45 cl

(c) 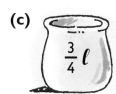 $\frac{3}{4} \ell$

(d) 20 cl

(e)  1 ℓ 9 cl

- **in centilitres.**

(f) 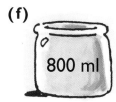 800 ml

(g)  0·5 ℓ

(h) 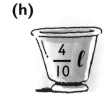 $\frac{4}{10} \ell$

(i)  $\frac{1}{4} \ell$

(j) 70 ml

2 What is the capacity of the container which
- holds more

(a)  0·3 ℓ  33 cl

(b) 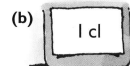 1 cl   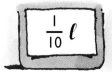 $\frac{1}{10} \ell$

- holds less?

(c)  832 ml    80 cl

(d)  55 ml    5 cl

3 Write in order.

(a) Start with the **largest** volume.

66 cl	$\frac{6}{10} \ell$	6 ℓ	606 ml	6 cl

(b) Start with the **smallest** volume.

13 ℓ	1 ℓ 3 cl	1·3 ℓ	1003 ml	133 cl

4 Which of these containers have a capacity greater than 35 cl and smaller than 65 cl?

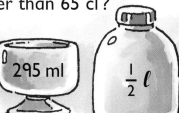 295 ml
 $\frac{1}{2} \ell$
 700 ml
 0·6 ℓ 400 ml

milk   water   olive oil   vinegar

88 cl   76 cl   85 cl   74 cl

1 Which scale shows the volume of the
  • milk   • water   • olive oil   • vinegar?

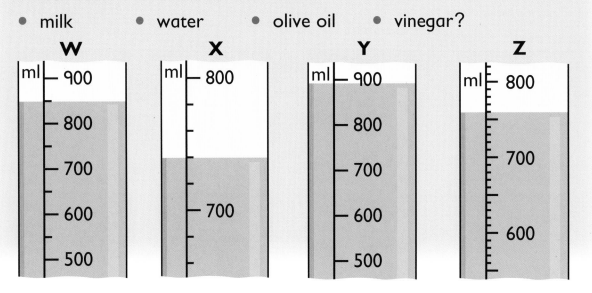

W   **X**   **Y**   **Z**

2

For each container in turn
  • estimate the capacity in centilitres   • check by measuring.
Record your results in a table like this.

Container	Estimate	Measure
A	about cl	about cl
B		

3 Find two other containers each with a capacity of between 35 cl and 0·5 ℓ.

1 Some children in class 6 have been pouring water into containers.

(a) Write True (T) or False (F) for each child's statement.

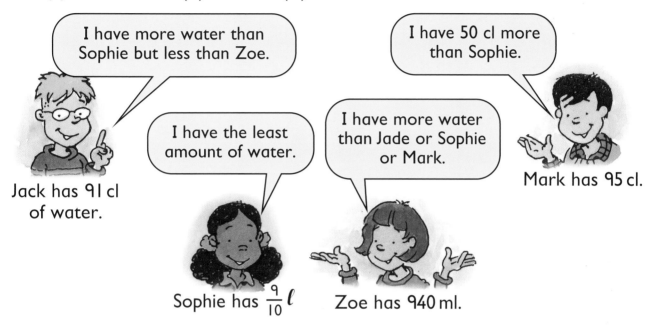

I have more water than Sophie but less than Zoe.

I have 50 cl more than Sophie.

I have the least amount of water.

I have more water than Jade or Sophie or Mark.

Mark has 95 cl.

Jack has 91 cl of water.

Sophie has $\frac{9}{10}\ell$

Zoe has 940 ml.

(b) What volume of water does each of these children have?

I have 75 ml less than Mark.

Rosie

I have 10 cl more than Sophie.

Leela

2

1450 ml   1·1 ℓ   70 cl   360 ml   0·8 ℓ   30 cl

What is the total volume of paint in these containers?

(a) green and yellow   **(b)** brown and white
(c) blue and brown   **(d)** yellow and red
(e) red and green   **(f)** blue, yellow and white.

3

45 cl $\frac{4}{10}\ell$ 35 cl   50 cl   550 ml

The sum of which two volumes is
(a) 900 ml   **(b)** 0·75 ℓ   **(c)** 1ℓ 50 ml   **(d)** 1ℓ?

MAGIC MOMENTS Birthday Cake mixture

raisins 150 g
apple slices 85 g
orange peel 65 g
flour 0·5 kg
butter 50 g

water 4 tablespoons **or** 68 ml

milk 5 cl

lemon juice 5 ml

Preheat oven to 375°F (190°C)

Bake mixture for a quarter of an hour

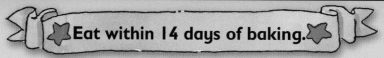

Eat within 14 days of baking.

1 Write, in kilograms, the total weight of **fruit** used in the cake mixture.

2 Find the difference between the weights of flour and fruit used.

3 What is the **total** volume of **liquid** used?

4 What quantity of water is there in 12 tablespoons?

5 How many tablespoons of water are needed to make 17 cl?

6 The oven takes about 20 minutes to reach a temperature of 190°C. For about how many minutes has it been switched on when the baking is **complete**?

7 The cake mixture is placed in the oven at 11.55am. At what time should it be removed?

8 Should a cake baked on 28th March be eaten on 12th April? Explain.

I litre is about 1¾ pints.

1 About how many **pints** of oxygen are in each tank?

(a) 2 *l*

(b) 100 *l*

(c) 12 *l*

(d) 4½ *l*

2 About how many **litres** are left in each fuel tank?

I gallon is about 4·5 litres.

(a) 10 gallons left

(b) 25 gallons left

(c) 150 gallons left

(d) 500 gallons left

3 I ounce is about 30 grams.

Write the approximate weight, **in grams,** of each moon rock.

(a) 4 ounces

(b) 7 ounces

(c) 12 ounces

(d) 10½ ounces

4 What is the approximate **total** weight, **in kilograms,** of these moon rocks?

300 g   4 ounces   250 g   11 ounces

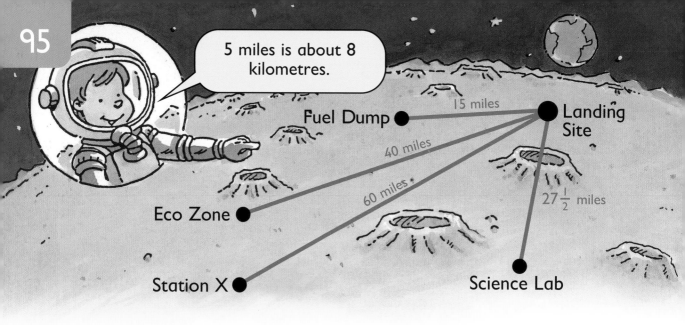

1 About how many **kilometres** is the distance from the Landing Site to

(a) Fuel Dump   (b) Eco Zone   (c) Station X   (d) Science Lab?

DISTANCES FROM STATION X

Crater	15 miles.............
Volcano	26 kilometres...
Dust Desert	36 kilometres...
Zircon Mine	21 miles.............

2

Which is nearer to Station X

(a) Crater or Volcano
(b) Zircon Mine or Dust Desert?

3 What is the approximate weight, **in pounds,** of each crate of machine parts?

1 kilogram is about 2·2 pounds

(a) 10 kg   (b) 8 kg   (c) 20 kg   (d) 15·5 kg

4 List the Imperial **and** metric units which would be best for measuring

(a) the capacity of a tea pot
(b) the weight of a calculator
(c) the distance from the Earth to the Moon
(d) the capacity of a car's fuel tank
(e) the weight of a brick.

1 **(a)** Copy each design on squared paper.
(b) Complete each design so that it has two lines of symmetry.

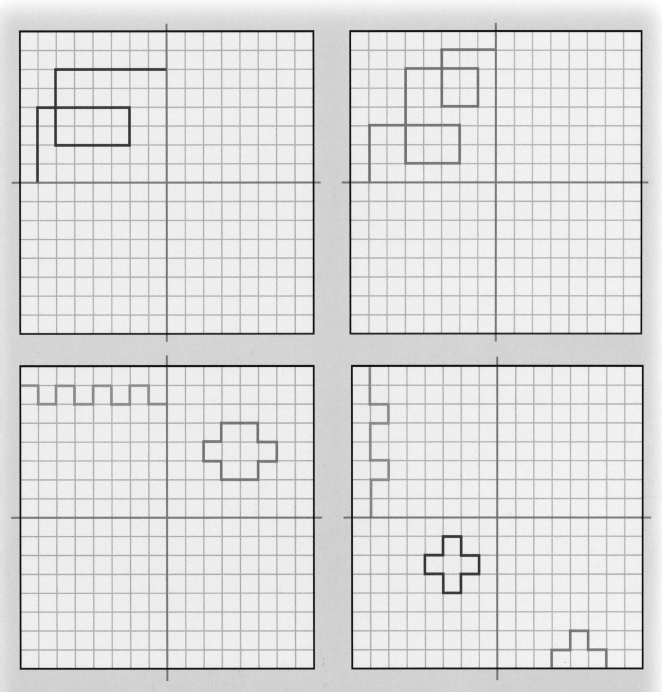

2 Draw and colour symetrical designs of your own.

1 (a) Cut out the shapes from the bottom half of Pupil Sheet 41.
  (b) Rotate each shape on top of its twin from the top half.
  (c) Write on each shape the number of times it fits its outline in one complete turn.
  (d) Stick the shapes in your exercise book.

2

  (a) Repeat question 1 for the shapes on Pupil Sheet 42.
  (b) Copy and complete a table like this:

Regular Polygon	Number of equal sides and equal angles	Number of times it fits its outline
Equilateral triangle	3	3

  (c) What do you notice?

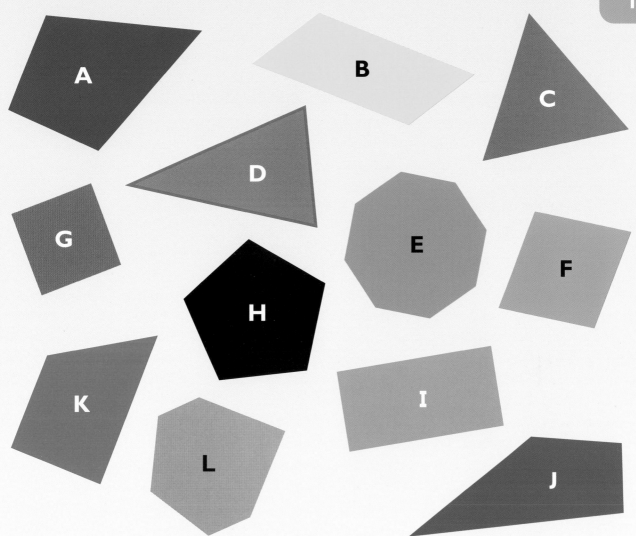

1 Which of the shapes

- **(a)** are quadrilaterals
- **(b)** have **all** sides equal
- **(c)** have **only one** pair of **opposite** sides parallel
- **(d)** has only one pair of opposite sides **equal**
- **(e)** have only **two pairs** of opposite sides equal **and** parallel
- **(f)** has more than two pairs of opposite sides equal and parallel
- **(g)** have only one pair of **adjacent** sides equal
- **(h)** are **not regular** and have only two pairs of adjacent sides equal
- **(i)** has one pair of opposite sides parallel but **not** equal
- **(j)** are parallelograms?

2 Name each shape.

1 Which of the shapes

    (a)   have no lines of symmetry

    (b)   have only one line of symmetry

    (c)   have only two lines of symmetry

    (d)   have more than two lines of symmetry?

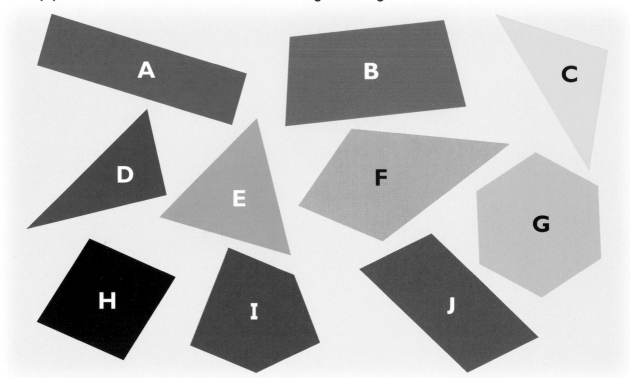

2 Which of the shapes

    (a)   have **all** angles equal   **(b)**   has **only** right angles

    (c)   has only obtuse angles   **(d)**   has only acute angles

    (e)   has only two right angles   **(f)**   has only one pair of equal angles

    (g)   has right, acute **and** obtuse angles

    (h)   has only one pair of **opposite** angles equal

    (i)   have no right angles and only two pairs of opposite angles equal

    (j)   has no right angles and only one pair of **adjacent** angles equal

    (k)   has **no** equal angles?

3 Name each of the shapes.

4 Use squared paper. Draw a shape which has

- two right angles
- four obtuse angles
- only one line of symmetry.

Use Tangram Pieces.

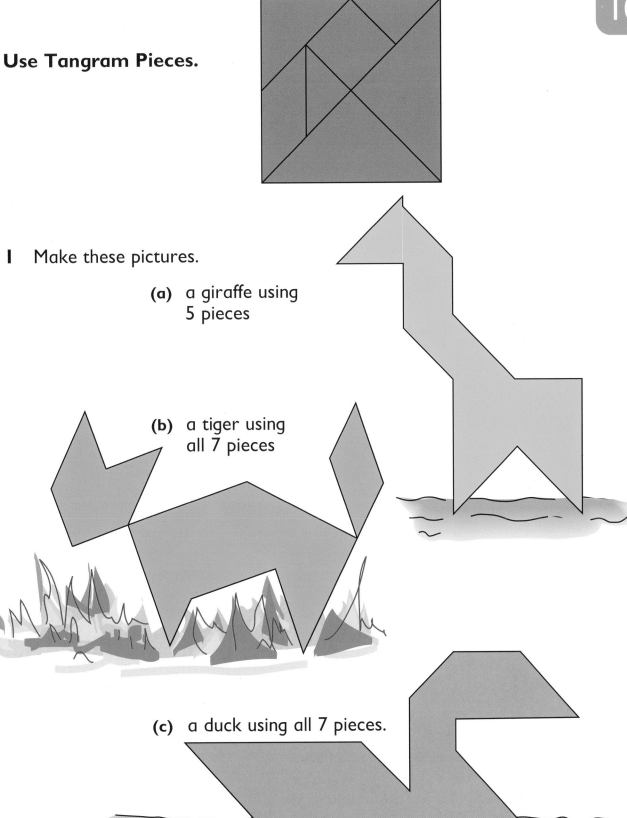

I Make these pictures.

      (a) a giraffe using
            5 pieces

      (b) a tiger using
            all 7 pieces

      (c) a duck using all 7 pieces.

2 Use Tangram pieces to make your own pictures.

1   **Use compasses and a ruler.**
   Make these circle patterns.

(a)

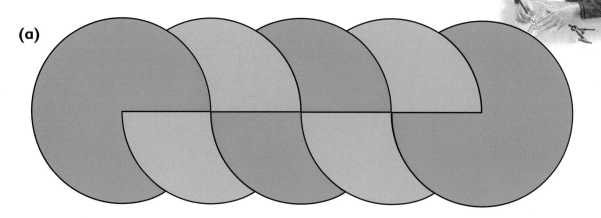

(b)

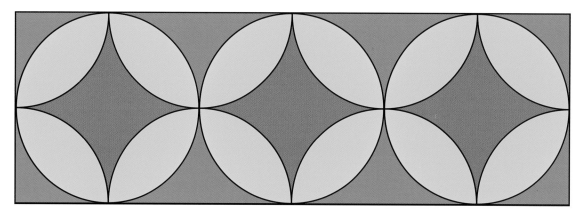

(c)

1 Start with **6 equally-spaced points on the circumference of a circle** each time. Make each of these designs.

(a)

(b)

2 Investigate other designs you can make starting with 6 equally-spaced points on the circumference of a circle.

1 Use linking squares. Find which of these are nets of a cube.

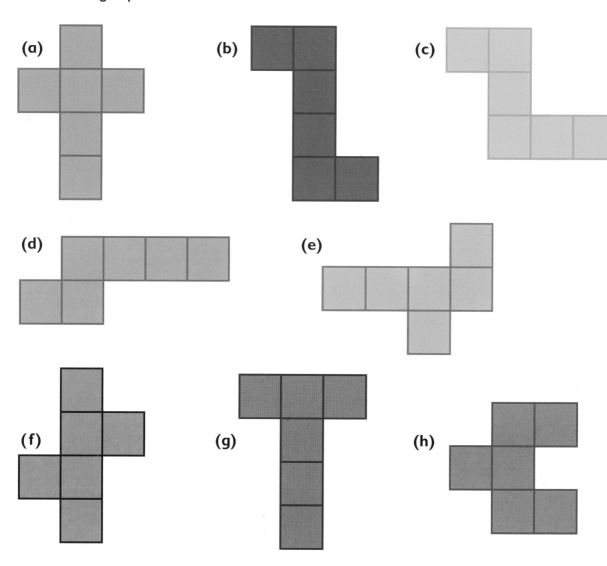

(a)

(b)

(c)

(d)

(e)

(f)

(g)

(h)

2 Join linking squares to make other nets of a cube.
Draw these other nets on squared paper.

SURFACE AREA

1 Calculate the total surface area of each shape.

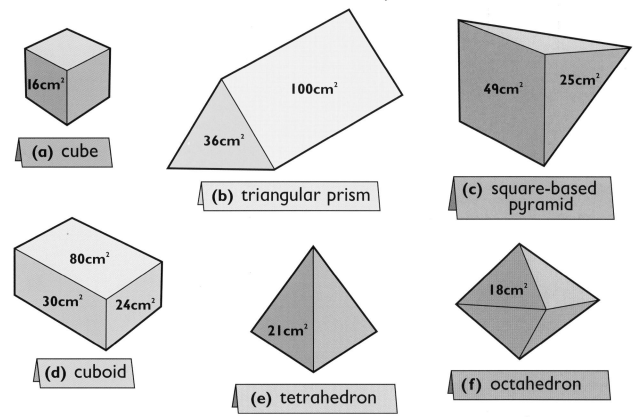

16cm²   **(a) cube**

100cm²   36cm²   **(b) triangular prism**

49cm²   25cm²   **(c) square-based pyramid**

80cm²   30cm²   24cm²   **(d) cuboid**

21cm²   **(e) tetrahedron**

18cm²   **(f) octahedron**

2 A 3D shape has

- 2 square faces, each with sides 3 cm long
- 4 rectangular faces, each with sides 5 cm long and 3 cm broad.

(a) Name the 3D shape.

(b) What is the **total surface area** of the shape in cm²?

3 The total surface area of a cube is 54 cm².
What is the total length of each of its edges?

In each question, check your answers, if you need to, by building shapes using linking cubes.

1 How many cubes **do you think** are needed to build each of these shapes?

(a)

(b)

(c)

(d)

2 What is the least number of cubes needed to make each of these shapes into a cuboid?

(a)

(b)

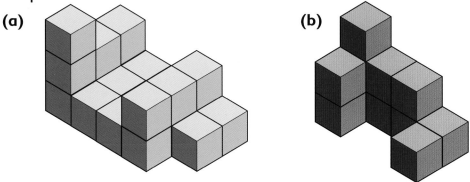

3 In each shape, what is the least number of cubes needed to **cover and join** the coloured faces?

(a)

(b)

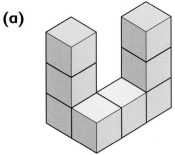

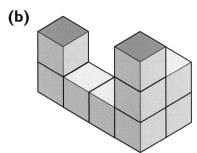

1 The yellow dot has co-ordinates (⁻4, 2).
What are the co-ordinates of the

(**a**) pink dot   (**b**) green dot   (**c**) red dot   (**d**) blue dot
(**e**) white dot   (**f**) black dot   (**g**) orange dot?

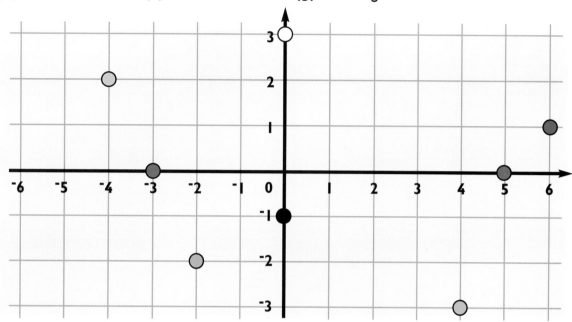

2 What colour is the dot at each of these positions?

(**a**) (3, 3)   (**b**) (0, 1)   (**c**) (6, ⁻1)   (**d**) (⁻3, ⁻3)   (**e**) (⁻5, 0)
(**f**) (2, ⁻2)   (**g**) (⁻6, 1)   (**h**) (0, 0)

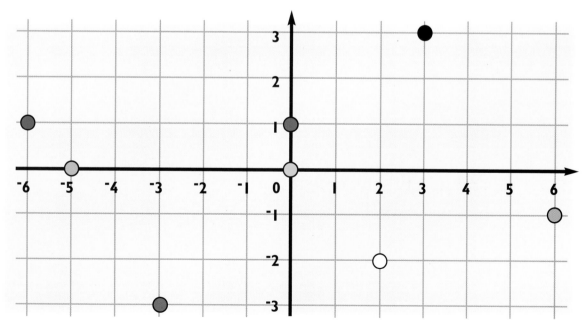

Trace each shape then flip to find reflections.

1 List the co-ordinates of
- the vertices of the half shape
- the vertices needed to complete the shape so that the **horizontal** axis is a line of symmetry.

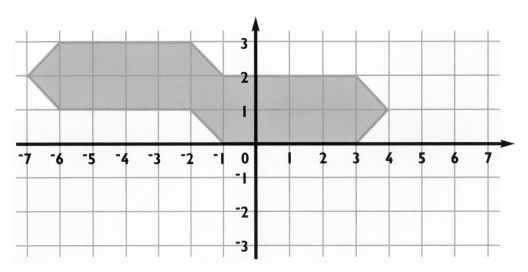

2 List the co-ordinates of
- the vertices of the shape
- the vertices of the shape's reflections when the horizontal **and** vertical axes are lines of symmetry.

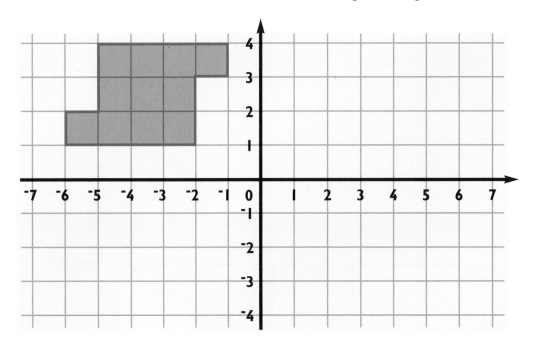

Use tracing paper if you need to.

1 List the co-ordinates of the vertices of each shape
  - in the position shown
  - after the shape has moved

(a) six units right　　　　　　**(b)** five units left

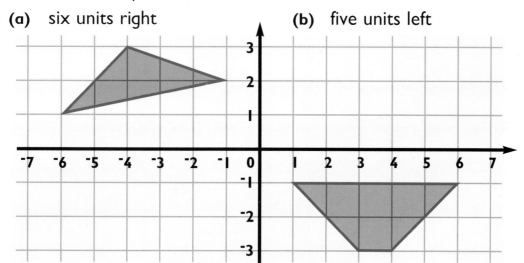

(c) eight units right **and**　　**(d)** six units left **and**
　　one unit up　　　　　　　　　two units down

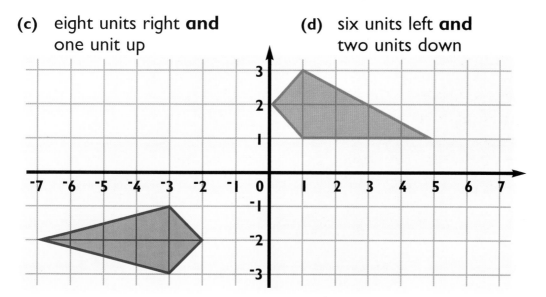

(e) five units right **and**　　　**(f)** seven units left **and**
　　two units down　　　　　　　two units up.

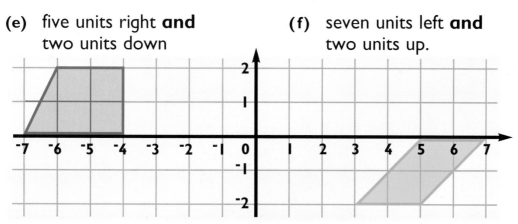

Trace each shape and rotate to find its new position.

I   List the co-ordinates of the vertices of each shape
- in the position shown
- after the shape has rotated about the vertex at (0, 0)

(a)   90° anti-clockwise

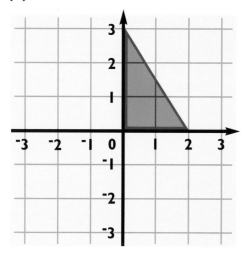

(b)   180° clockwise

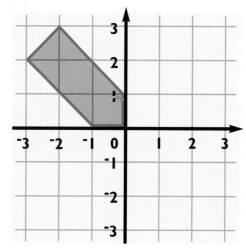

(c)   90° clockwise

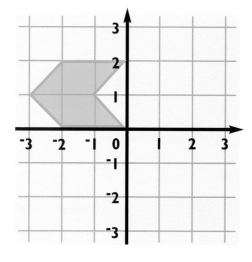

(d)   180° anti-clockwise.

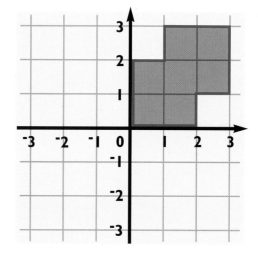

1 Which angles are • acute • obtuse • reflex?

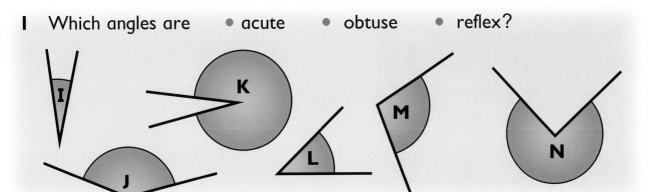

2 (a) Estimate the size of angle **P** then check by measuring with a protractor **to the nearest degree**.

(b) Repeat, in turn, for angles **Q**, **R**, **S**, **T** and **U**.

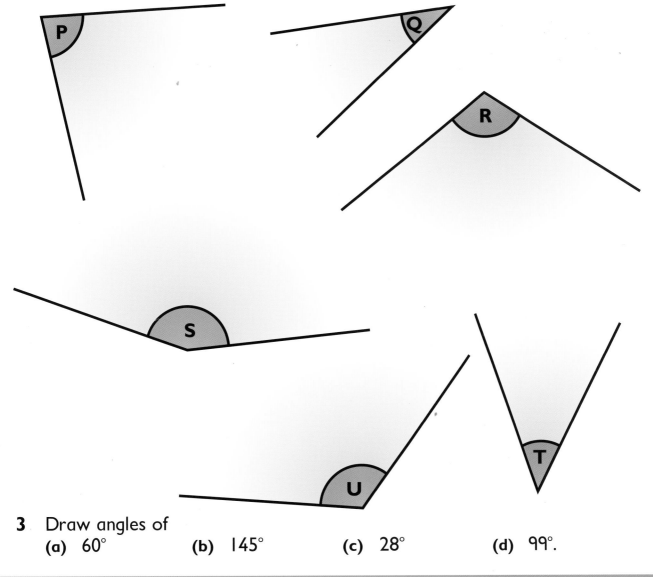

3 Draw angles of
(a) 60°   (b) 145°   (c) 28°   (d) 99°.

1 **Calculate** the size of each red angle.

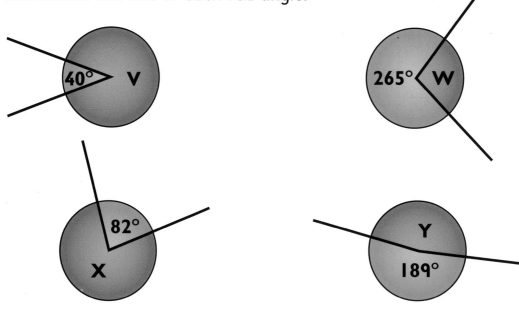

40° V

265° W

82°
X

Y
189°

2 Calculate the size of each blue angle.

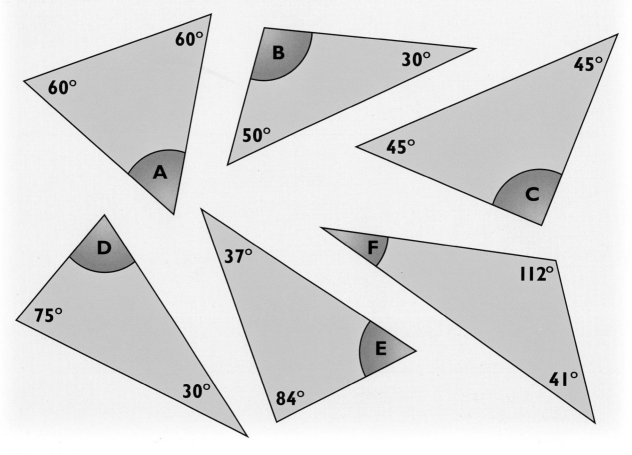

60°

60°

A

B

30°

50°

45°

45°

C

D

75°

37°

F

112°

E

30°

84°

41°

The **trend graph** shows the number of swimmers at Parkvale Pool at 9 am each day for two weeks.

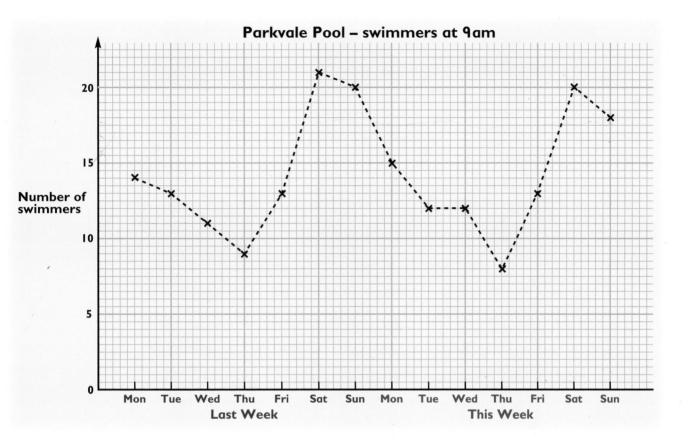

Parkvale Pool – swimmers at 9am

1   On which day and in which week was the number of swimmers

   (a) greatest   **(b)** smallest   **(c)** eleven   **(d)** eighteen?

2   How many swimmers were there on

   (a) Thursday last week   **(b)** Friday this week?

3   Write about the **trend** shown by the graph.

4   This table shows the number of swimmers who bought a ticket during each one hour session on Monday this week.

Time of session	09.00 -10.00	10.00 -11.00	11.00 -12.00	12.00 -13.00	13.00 -14.00	14.00 -15.00	15.00 -16.00	16.00 -17.00
Number of swimmers	15	18	16	38	35	21	9	23

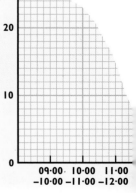

   (a) Draw a trend graph using the data.
   (b) Write about the trend shown by the graph.

1 The children in the Class 6 Red team find out how many times they can bounce a basketball in one minute.

Alan	Bindu	Dave	Sammy	Dion	Anne	Luke
48	51	51	55	56	57	60

(a) Name the children who bounced the ball the smallest and the greatest number of times and give the **range.**

(b) Name the children who bounced the ball the most common number of times and give the **mode.**

(c) Name the child whose number of bounces was in the middle of the order and give the **median.**

2 These are the Green team's results.

| 54 | 62 | 55 | 58 | 60 | 50 | 60 |

(a) Write the numbers of bounces in order.

(b) Find • the range • the mode • the median.

3 These are the results for the 11 children in the Blue team.

60	54	52	49	52	60
	57	58	50	60	64

(a) Write the numbers of bounces in order.

(b) Find • the range • the mode • the median.

4 (a) Write all 25 results for the red, green and blue teams in order.

(b) Find • the range • the mode • the median.

The Class 6 Red team measure the height they can make a ball bounce. The results are shown in the **bar chart**.

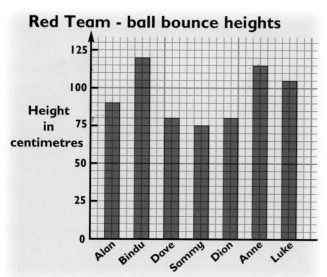

Red Team - ball bounce heights

Height in centimetres

1 Who made the ball bounce **(a)** highest **(b)** lowest?

2 For the Red team's results give
(a) the range **(b)** the mode **(c)** the median.

3 Each time the ball is thrown into the netball basket 3 points are scored. The points scored in one minute by the Green team were:

30   21   15   30   27   30   15

For the Green team's results, find
(a) the range **(b)** the mode **(c)** the median.

4 For each of these teams' results, find
(a) the range **(b)** the mode **(c)** the median.

Red team	Yellow team	Orange team
18 18 21 27 24 18 21	21 30 24 24 15 18 15 18 24	12 21 24 18 9 21 12 9 18 12 6 21 12

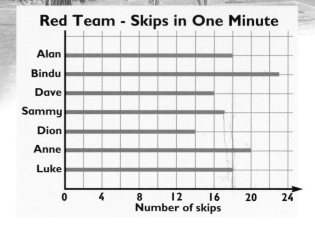

The **bar line chart** shows how many times the Class 6 Red team skipped in one minute.

1
(a) How many skips were made by • Anne • Sammy?
(b) Find the total number of skips for the whole team.
(c) Find the **mean** number of skips by dividing the total number of skips by the number of children in the team.
(d) Name the children whose number of skips was
• less than the mean • greater than the mean • equal to the mean.

2
(a) Find the total number of skips for the Green team.
(b) Calculate the mean number of skips per child.
(c) Name the children whose number of skips was
• above the mean • below the mean.

> **Green Team - Skips in One Minute**
> Steve - 22   Lisa - 20   Paul - 18
> Nazir - 15   Dianne - 21
> Joan - 17   Sheena - 20

3

These are the numbers of skips for the Blue team.

> 18 17 24 23
> 19 18 24
> 17 22 20 18

(a) What is • the range • the mode • the median?
(b) Find the mean number of skips per child.
(c) For **how many** children was the number of skips
• above the mean • below the mean • equal to the mean?

1 This **compound bar chart** shows the values of the book tokens given to five girls on their birthdays.

Birthday Book Tokens

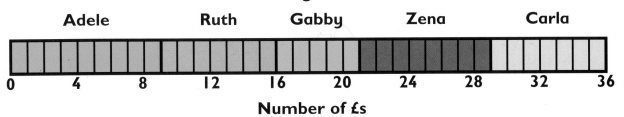

Number of £s

(a) What is the total value of the girls' book tokens?

(b) What is the value of the book token given to
- Adele • Carla • Gabby • Zena • Ruth?

(c) What fraction of the total value is the value of Adele's token?

(d) Use $\frac{1}{2}$-centimetre squared paper. Draw a **bar line chart** to show the same information as the compound bar chart.

2 These two graphs show the same information about the values of the gift vouchers given to five boys on their birthdays.

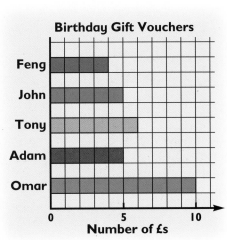

Birthday Gift Vouchers

Number of £s

(a) What is the total value of the vouchers?

(b) Whose voucher is $\frac{1}{3}$ of the total value?

(c) Which children's vouchers are of equal value?

(d) What is the value of each boy's voucher?

3 For each part of question **2**, which graph shows the answer more clearly?

Baxdale School's Shoebox Project helps to provide classroom items for schools in developing countries.

The children in Class 6 calculate the amount of money each group needs to collect to fill a shoebox with classroom items.

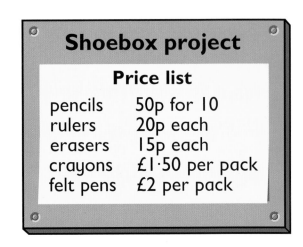

Shoebox project

Price list

pencils	50p for 10
rulers	20p each
erasers	15p each
crayons	£1·50 per pack
felt pens	£2 per pack

Red

pencils	60
rulers	30
erasers	60
crayons	12 packs
felt pens	10 packs

Yellow

pencils	90
rulers	60
erasers	30
crayons	10 packs
felt pens	12 packs

Blue

pencils	120
rulers	45
erasers	45
crayons	6 packs
felt pens	5 packs

Green

pencils	100
rulers	60
erasers	60
crayons	5 packs
felt pens	6 packs

Use the Spreadsheets on Pupil Sheet DH1.

1 **(a)** Complete a table like this for each of the four groups.

group	pencils	rulers	erasers	crayons	felt pens	
Number						
Cost each						**Total**
Total cost						

(b) Which group needs to collect • most money • least money?

(c) There are 5 children in each group. Find the mean amount of money that needs to be collected per child in each group.

2 The Red and Blue groups decide to change the contents of their shoeboxes.

The Red group wants
- 20 more pencils
- 20 fewer erasers.

The Blue group wants
- 40 fewer pencils
- 5 more packs of felt pens.

(a) Alter your tables to include this information.
(b) Find the mean amount of money that needs to be collected per child in • the Red group • the Blue group.

3 The Yellow and Green groups each add an extra item to their shoebox.

The Yellow group adds 8 tubes of paint at £1·75 each.
The Green group adds 12 glue sticks at £1·25 each.

Alter your tables to include this information.

	Svensun 5	Morten	Rodex	Sherwood
Talk time	300 min	130 min	180 min	300 min
Number of ring tones	21	43	20	24
Internet access	✓	no access	no access	✓ ✓
Accessories	✓	✓ ✓	✓	✓ ✓

	Quad	Venta	Norlund	Svensun 12
Talk time	210 min	210 min	240 min	480 min
Number of ring tones	14	48	35	20
Internet access	✓	✓	✓	✓
Accessories	✓	✓ ✓	✓ ✓ ✓	✓

Key :

Internet access			Accessories		
built in	with cable	with modem	hands free	new covers	fun pack

1 Name the mobile telephone models which

 (a) have exactly 210 minutes of talk time
 (b) have between 225 minutes and 325 minutes of talk time
 (c) have more than 40 different ring tones
 (d) have no access to the Internet
 (e) can access the Internet with a modem
 (f) can have new covers attached.

2 Which accessory is available with every one of the phones?

3 Which phone model has all the features listed?

(a) M.P.S.
 • exactly 20 ring tones
 • a hands-free kit
 • Internet access

(b) M.P.S.
 • exactly 35 ring tones
 • Internet access
 • new covers

(c) M.P.S.
 • access to the Internet with a cable attached
 • more than 22 ring tones
 • exactly 300 minutes of talk time

4 Ask your teacher if you can enter the information into a computer database.

Is it true that five eighths of the children in Year 6 are between 139 centimetres and 160 centimetres tall?

Some children carry out a survey to find the answer to their Headteacher's challenge question.

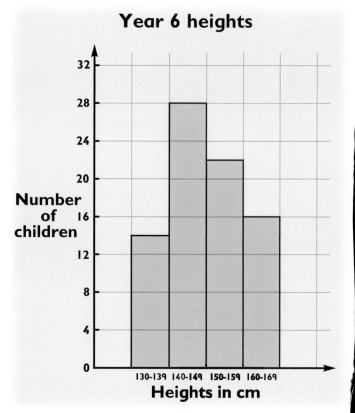

Year 6 heights

Number of children

Heights in cm

1 **(a)** How many class intervals are there in the graph?

(b) Which class interval contains
- the greatest number of children
- the smallest number of children

(c) In which class interval is
- the shortest height
- the tallest height?

(d) How many children are
- shorter than 140 cm
- between 149 cm and 160 cm tall?

(e) What fraction of the children are
- taller than 159 cm
- between 139 cm and 150 cm tall?

(f) What is **your** answer to the Headteacher's challenge question? Explain.

2 Use Pupil Sheet DH2.

Find out if five eighths of the children in **your** class are between 139 cm and 160 cm tall by
- measuring their heights to the nearest centimetre
- completing the frequency table
- drawing a bar chart of the data.

Data handling: bar charts with class intervals

I Your class is going on a trip to the seashore.

Use | impossible | **or** | unlikely | **or** | likely | **or** | certain |

to describe the likelihood of each of these events happening.

(a) You will see a crab.

(b) You will build a sandcastle 100 metres tall.

(c) The sea water will be salty.

(d) You will see a whale.

2 Draw a scale like this.

no chance   poor chance   even chance   good chance   certain

Draw and label arrows on your scale to show the chance of each of these events happening tomorrow.

(a)

It will snow.

(b)

You will eat lunch.

(c)

The first baby born will be a boy.

(d)

You will find a £20 note.

3 Suggest an event which

(a) is impossible   **(b)** is likely   **(c)** has an even chance of happening.

1 List all the possible outcomes if the arrow sticks to a card with

   (a) an odd number
   (b) a multiple of 4
   (c) a square number
   (d) a prime number.

2 List all the possible outcomes if the fish caught shows

   (a) an even number
   (b) a multiple of 3
   (c) a factor of 12
   (d) a triangular number.

3 What is the probability of rolling a die to give

   (a) a two
   (b) an odd number
   (c) a number less than 5
   (d) a number between 0 and 10?

4 Sally sells one hundred raffle tickets numbered 1 to 100.

Use │ less than one in two │ **or** │ one in two │ **or** │more than one in tw

to describe the probability of each of these events happening.

   (a) The winning ticket is a multiple of 5.
   (b) The winning ticket is an even number.